LIGHT IN MY
DARKEST NIGHT

By the same author

Adventures in Prayer
Beyond Our Selves
A Closer Walk
The Helper
Julie
Meeting God at Every Turn
My Personal Prayer Diary
Something More

LIGHT IN MY DARKEST NIGHT

Catherine Marshall

HODDER & STOUGHTON
LONDON SYDNEY AUCKLAND TORONTO

British Library Cataloguing in Publication Data

Marshall, Catherine, 1914–1983
  Light in my darkest night.
  1. Christian life – Devotional works
  I. Title
  242

  ISBN 0 340 52341 7

Published by Hodder and Stoughton, a division of Hodder and Stoughton Ltd, Mill Road, Dunton Green, Sevenoaks, Kent TN13 2YA. Editorial Office: 47 Bedford Square, London WC1B 3DP.

Printed in Great Britain by Cox & Wyman Ltd., Reading.

To Amy Catherine Marshall
whose time on earth touched many lives

With Gratitude _____

Deepest appreciation goes to Theresa Mulligan, whose computer expertise and research skills solved countless problems; to Elaine Brink for invaluable typing and secretarial help; to Steven Payne, O.C.D., the editor of the Catholic quarterly *Spiritual Life* magazine, for reading the manuscript and making helpful suggestions.

Once again I pay special tribute to Elizabeth (Tib) Sherrill, who has provided priceless editorial help on Marshall-LeSourd books now for 28 years. Because of her love for Catherine, Catherine's family, and the LeSourds, Tib worked on this book as if it were her own.

Finally, gratitude to the sixteen prayer warriors who gathered at Cape Cod in the summer of 1971, all of whom have been supportive and cooperative—and especially to all those family members who not only helped guide this project, but also contributed their written observations and experiences of that memorable period.

Contents

Editor's Foreword

*C*atherine Marshall LeSourd's *Light in My Darkest Night* has been waiting to be written for the past seventeen years. Catherine always intended to do it herself, but somehow the time never seemed right. As the years passed, I wondered whether the events of a profoundly significant phase of her life—and mine—would ever be told.

Yet as time went by, the story not only did not die, it kept arising in conversations with friends and family: "Remember the summer of 1971? . . . So many lives were touched. . . . How long did it take Catherine to get over it? . . . Where has Catherine written about it?"

The answer to that last question is—nowhere.

Except for tantalizing fragments in *Something More* and

Meeting God at Every Turn, this central crisis of her life remained concealed, segments of it known to family and close friends, portions of it poured out in her journals, the basic pain and frustration of it known by me chiefly through the dialogues the two of us had together.

There are two reasons why I'm convinced that Catherine would have wanted this book published. First, Catherine had a deep sense of mission about her life. She felt that God had called her to write, that she was to be fearless and selfless about revealing her spiritual valleys—as well as the mountaintops—to her readers. Early in her career she realized that God used her weaknesses more than her strengths as teaching points. Not many Christian writers have bared their souls with such transparent honesty as Catherine did in her books. This book especially reflects this sense of personal candor.

And second, the subject has a special urgency today. Christians today are going through periods of darkness, where even the certainty of the Light's existence is lost. There is tremendous need for teaching on how to survive these dark nights. Now is God's moment for this message, I believe. Perhaps this is why He did not give Catherine a "go" on this book before.

To tell the full story it is necessary to go back to some pre-1971 episodes, to pick up roots of conflicts that came to a head that year. In every dark night of the soul there are contributing factors that go back many years, sometimes many generations. My hope is that readers of this book who are going through dark times themselves will be encouraged to trace similar threads in their own lives. To some, the circumstances that contributed to Catherine's crisis of faith may not seem as dire or tragic as their own; others may find their troubles pale in comparison to Catherine's. Whatever the landscape of your particular valley, the truths that Catherine learned as she traveled hers are valid for all.

The structure of this book follows the pattern set by *A Closer Walk*: Most of the material comes from Catherine's own writings and journals, with background information and comments by me. In addition, I have drawn on twenty hours of tapes that Catherine and I made together in the fall of 1971, recording our recollections of, and reactions to, the tumultuous events of the preceding summer. Also important are reflections from other leading characters in the story: Peter and Edith Marshall, my daughter Linda Le-Sourd Lader, John and Elizabeth Sherrill, Virginia Lively, Jamie Buckingham.

Doing this book has been painful for me, yet also richly rewarding. I have had to go back in time to read, as Catherine read, accounts of the dark nights that earlier Christians went through. I've had to probe my memory and our files for missing pieces of the story. Out of it all has come a better understanding of Catherine that has made me cherish her memory more than ever. Also have come insights about myself. What a mixture of strengths and weaknesses we all are! Catherine's central message: *If we will let Him, the Lord will help us grow strong precisely in the weak places themselves.*

Catherine let Him. She went through a dark night experience that shook her faith and tested all her resources. It involved all-out spiritual warfare, not only for Catherine but for family members and friends.

My prayer is that the discoveries in this book will be a shaft of light into the minds and hearts of hurting people who do not understand why God seems to have abandoned them. Everywhere one turns today, there is a cry of pain, an anguished word of despair. Many are wandering in a personal darkness that renders them helpless and defeated. They desperately need to know there is a way toward the light.

For the good news that Catherine discovered was that God had not abandoned her; He had only withdrawn for a

season . . . *in order to bring her into a still closer relationship with Himself.*

If you identify with Catherine's dark night of the soul, you
can also look forward with confidence to the sunlit heights
of a new and stronger faith. That's the bright promise of this
book.

Leonard E. LeSourd
Evergreen Farm
Lincoln, Virginia

Light in My Darkest Night

Section I

Gathering Shadows

The Winter
of '49 _____

*C*atherine . . . Peter Marshall's death from a heart attack at
age 46 was a devastating blow. "Why?" I asked the Lord.
"Why take a man who loves You so much, who is in the
prime time of life, whose impact on people *for You* is so
great?" In the midst of grief, I had a million "whys."

Not one of them was answered. Instead, into my anguished emotions there crept one morning a strange, all-
pervading peace. Through and around me flowed love as I
had never before experienced it. It was as if Someone who
loved me very much were wrapping me 'round and 'round
with His infinite care and protection.

I knelt there marveling at what was happening. I had done nothing, said nothing, to bring it about. I understood no more than before the *reason* for my young husband's death. I only knew that in some way that transcended reason, it was deeply and eternally all right. Into my mind came a verse from the Bible, "Underneath are the everlasting arms." That described what I was feeling.

I opened my New Testament and found these strength-imparting words:

> So, up with your listless hands! Strengthen your weak knees! And make straight paths for your feet to walk in. . . .

> Hebrews 12:11–12, MOFFATT

Soon afterward I was led to begin writing my husband's biography, *A Man Called Peter.*

I had asked God to tell me Why? He gave me no answer to this question. Instead, He gave me

. . . infinite Love for my present need,

. . . step-by-step guidance for my future walk.

How much anguish I might have saved myself twenty years later if I had remembered this! If I'd thought back to the time of this first great bereavement, when instead of explanations, He gave me Himself.

The Decision _____

*C*atherine ... With the success of *A Man Called Peter* a new world opened up for me. My goal now was to communicate to others the excitement I felt for the living Lord.

The decade of the 1950s was one of much creativity—and much loneliness. I was not prepared at age 34, when widowhood began for me, to be a single parent to our son, Peter John, to manage my finances, and to handle a strenuous career of speaking and writing. There had been no training for any of this. At the time of Peter's death, I had been driving an automobile for only three months.

Yet in my weakness I discovered His strength. I needed Jesus every day, seeking Him in my morning time before all else.

And then after ten years of widowhood, I met Leonard LeSourd, the forty-year-old editor of *Guideposts* magazine. I liked Len's creative approach to publishing, his strong commitment to Jesus Christ, and the resourceful way he pursued me. In fact, for the first time since meeting Peter I was flushed with the joy of romance.

With a succession of housekeepers, Len had been struggling to rear three small children from a previous marriage. With Peter John now "out of the nest" and attending college, I had to decide if I was ready to take on full-time mothering again.

In my morning times that still, small Voice in my inner spirit asked me some searching questions:

> Have you counted the cost? Have you really looked at the readjustments necessary for another marriage?
>
> Are there not certain areas of your life where rigidity is creeping in? The rough and tumble of family life is My antidote to rigidity. But are you willing to be cured?
>
> And do you not realize that My way would be to send you a man not just to satisfy your own needs, but because he has gigantic needs himself?

The issue was whether I was ready for that much commitment, not just to a man, but to three children too. Part of me was excited and stirred; the other part wanted to flee.

Both Len and I were agreed on the need to put Jesus at the center of any remarriage. Still I hung back. . . .

I thought with longing of the new house being built for me in Washington. It was almost finished. Adjoining my bedroom, cut off from the rest of the house, would be a step-down room where I could write. It would be my sanctuary. I was most reluctant to give up that prospect. Still, I would live in that house alone except for those brief holiday times when Peter John would be home from college.

Two roads stretched ahead, and I was at the parting of the

ways. In that house being built I might produce many articles and books. There I would have a cushioned, sheltered life—yes, and probably a lonely one.

And, if I chose the other road, I would plunge directly back into turbulent life. It would mean being a mother to Jeffrey, a mischievous imp of three; to Chester, six, with enormous brown eyes full of questions; to Linda, ten, approaching the challenging years of adolescence—and I had had no experience in rearing a daughter.

"Lord," I prayed one September morning in 1959, "I don't understand at all. Are You in this?"

I took a deep breath, for there was a sudden luminosity about this moment that I recognized. It had happened before when I asked Him for understanding. Once again, no illumination came to my mind. Instead, there was the overwhelming sense of His presence.

A bracing presence! No harp strings and angel choruses—this was no rosy-cloud vision. It was more like being slapped in the face with a wet washcloth. Or like being brought to earth with a thud and bidden to stand on one's feet.

Suddenly, the choice God was presenting to me was clear. To say yes to this man I loved, taking his children into my heart and life, meant a difficult adjustment. Yet I saw that if I said no and chose the other road, I would be turning away from the mainstream of life. The "no" way would be comfortable, but it would take me farther and farther from contact with people—and, ultimately, from God who shapes us through the people He places in our path.

At that moment His command seemed clear—"Say yes to life."

The Shadow _____

*L*en . . . I understood Catherine's struggle over whether to wed again, especially when three young children came with the package. Yet I confidently expected her to receive a "go" from the Lord to marry me. Why would He tell me one thing and Catherine another?

Six months before, I had been in a period of deep discouragement, trying to fill the role of single parent while commuting 75 miles from Carmel, New York, to my Manhattan job as executive editor of *Guideposts* magazine. My prayer was a most simple and direct one—"Lord, would You guide me to the woman You have selected to share my life?"

The first name dropped into my mind after this prayer

was Catherine's. I couldn't have been more surprised. I had met Catherine Marshall several years before when I had asked her to write an article for *Guideposts*. She did—coincidentally on the subject of "How to Find God's Guidance."

"Lord, can You be telling me that Catherine is Your choice as my wife?"

Silence. Nothing about it seemed to make sense, and I was far from experienced in asking for and receiving guidance from God. Still I figured I had nothing to lose by going to Washington, D.C., to see her. So we set up a date for a Saturday in August.

Catherine and I have described our courtship in previous books.[1] My main surprise was not only how we meshed together with our ideas and convictions, but the degree of physical attraction we had as well.

On that August Saturday we took a picnic lunch up to Skyline Drive in western Virginia and talked for ten straight hours, discovering what a lot we had in common. We were both PK's (preachers' kids), her father Presbyterian, mine Methodist. We came from strong, close-knit families. (Both sets of parents had marriages that were to last more than fifty years.) God had gifted us both with a love of words, Catherine as a writer, me as an editor. At that time we were both single parents.

One place where Catherine and I differed was in the timing of our Christian commitment. She met the Lord as a teenager, where I had resisted Him, seeking adventure in sports and as an Air Corps pilot during World War II. Like so many men of my time I had considered Jesus "loving but weak"—prejudiced, I think, by Sunday school pictures portraying Him as effeminate and unaggressive.

As a boy of twelve I had once cried in a sad movie and was so embarrassed by this show of emotion before my

---

[1] Catherine in *Meeting God at Every Turn*, I in *A Closer Walk*.

peers that I gave myself an order: "You will never cry again." In essence, I was telling myself not to feel strongly about anything or anyone. I didn't, either, until I was 29, becoming along the way shallow, self-centered, dead of spirit—a frozen man.

The thaw began in May 1948 at a weekend retreat for a group of young adults from the Marble Collegiate Church in New York City. I had gone to this group originally looking for a date. Somewhat against my will I went to the retreat, was annoyed to discover that my emotions were being touched at a deep level. Late Saturday night I found myself kneeling at the chapel altar below a virile picture of Jesus, where I surrendered my life to Him. The tears, dammed up for so many years, flowed.

It was at this same church that I met beautiful, talented Eve. Though I realized even as we were dating that she had a problem with alcohol, I felt naively that we could work this out once we were married. For I was ready now to settle down. Eve was not only a believer but a leader in our young adult group. Surely the love of God and our love for each other would see us over any rough places.

Eve and I were married at Marble Collegiate, had three children in seven years. The alcohol problem was kept in check as long as we lived in New York City close to our Christian friends. When we moved 75 miles to the country, the internal pressures on Eve seemed to explode.

Eve had counsel from psychiatrists and pastors, therapy at a treatment center. As her condition worsened, she was hospitalized for seven months. Later, her father, a physician in the Midwest, committed her temporarily to a state institution. Nothing seemed to help. After ten years of marriage, "for the sake of the children" we divorced.

For me it was a complete and senseless tragedy. In helpless frustration over a five-year period I watched the life of the woman I loved deteriorate. Never had I even imagined such pain, such grief. It precipitated a crisis of faith. "Why,

Lord, would You let this happen to me? I've tried to be a good husband, a good Christian," was my self-righteous, rebellious plea.

God was silent. I've learned since that He has a way of giving those who belong to Him a long leash. So I turned my back on Him, tried to rediscover life in the fast lane. It didn't take much time for me to fall on my face. The attempt to resume my old lifestyle was a disaster for me and bad for the children.

When I came back to Him on my knees, repentant, He was merciful. That was when, in response to my prayer for a new life partner, the name *Catherine Marshall* popped into my mind.

Catherine shared with her readers on several occasions the problems she faced adjusting to the idea of mothering my three young children. She confronted another, graver concern, however, one which, out of respect for Eve and me, she wrote about only in her journals: marrying a divorced man.

Hadn't Jesus Himself expressly forbidden it?

> But I say to you that whoever divorces his wife for any reason except sexual immorality causes her to commit adultery; and whoever marries a woman who is divorced commits adultery.
>
> Matthew 5:32, NKJ

Catherine and I discussed the situation in depth, talked with Christian counselors and pastors . . . receiving a bewildering variety of opinions. Catherine agonized over this, praying about it for weeks.

Finally she shared with me the word she believed she had received: *The Lord is in the business of restoring broken homes and healing damaged families. He hates divorce, as He hates all sin, for the harm it does in every life it touches. But He does not lock us into our sins; He is the God of redemption and new beginnings.*

At that time Catherine was serving as woman's editor for a Christian magazine. When our engagement was announced, the publisher flew to Washington and met with Catherine to express his concern. "Your Christian readers will be greatly upset if you marry a divorced man," he told her.

More anguish for Catherine, as she weighed not only her own possible flouting of God's law, but the harm it might do to others. In the end, though, she placed her trust in her understanding of the Lord as the One who ever wills to bind up what is broken.

Catherine and I were married on November 14, 1959, with both our pastor-fathers officiating, along with our mutual friend Dr. Norman Vincent Peale.

With the wedding, however, the divorce issue did not go away.

A New Life

*C*atherine, February 1960 ... Lord, I find myself surprised to be where I am this morning, looking out over a snow-covered backyard, hearing new noises in a strange house. Soon I will be busy getting two children off to school on the bus, driving a third to nursery school.

I am adjusting once again to a man's schedule. He catches an eight o'clock train to the city and his office at *Guideposts*. Love has come a second time, only this time I'm being asked to love three children as well. Loving Len comes naturally—he's warm, open, patient, giving. With the children—I'm making progress.

Home for us all is a sprawling white house with red shutters set in the rocky, tree-shaded countryside of Westchester County. Our town of Chappaqua is about forty miles north of New York City.

Two *Guideposts* editors, John and Elizabeth Sherrill, are neighbors. They also have three young children, close to the ages of our three; I can already see that our lives and those of the Sherrills will become closely entwined.

Daily Len and I are making new discoveries—new to us, at least—about You in relation to marriage and family life. That's why when the automatic coffeepot attached to our clock starts percolating each morning, we're beginning to anticipate rather than dread this early rising. We read Your Word, share our discoveries, then pray together.

This morning, we identified three very definite ways that You lift love and romance to a higher level:

The first is that You are able and eager to guide us into a satisfying emotional life, *if we will rid ourselves of the falsehood that You want to take away our fun.* Only You can reach deep enough to touch our emotions and bring them fully alive, balancing seriousness with a sense of humor, keeping play and passion in juxtaposition.

Secondly, love is a gift and You can give this gift only to those who are willing *to keep their hearts open.* To keep the heart open means running the risk of getting hurt; thus, we must trust You before we can truly experience love.

Finally, there is a joyous surprise in discovering You as the One who *steps up the voltage of physical attraction.* When You said, "I am come that they might have life," You didn't mean just spiritual life, but all of life. We sense that when the edge is gone off any part of living, then the spirit in us is growing dim.

So we have concluded that You are far more concerned with human love than we had realized. And learning day by day about love—both human and divine—absorbs us.

Lord, my prayer this morning is that I stay constantly in Your will. Guide me, protect me, sustain me, Lord, in all that I do and particularly now with my new family.

Spring 1960 . . . Len and I together have just prayed for our neighbor, John Sherrill, Lord. John received bad news yesterday from his doctor. A growth in his neck requires immediate surgery: two years ago an operation in the same area disclosed malignant melanoma.

Since Len and I are editorial associates with John and his wife, Tib, we have gotten to know them very well. They're intelligent, highly educated, endlessly curious about the world around them, and I think that's their problem. The diversity of religious experience is what fascinates them. They roam the length and breadth of this country seeking stories for *Guideposts*, interviewing people, ghost-writing their experiences . . . always *other people's* experiences. I think their oh-so-professional "objectivity" is a defense against letting faith get too personal.

This morning I'm sensing that our prayers for John's healing are not the end of my involvement. Suddenly John's crisis seems to be my crisis—part of my "bundle" of responsibility, as the Quakers express it. So, what is my next step since Len is already on his way to work?

A series of thoughts keep pounding at me: healing is not an end in itself; it is a dividend of the Gospel. Physical health is but one part of total wholeness. Then this—has John ever made an act of turning his whole being over to You, Lord?

Who am I to ask John a question like that? He's written about total commitment—other people's commitment—over and over. I'm sure the usual religious clichés would be repugnant to him. Considering all this, would not any question about his relationship to God be gross presumption on my part and anathema to him?

Yet, time is running out. Only 24 hours remain until John enters New York's Memorial Hospital for surgery. What he thinks of me does not matter at a time like this. The fact that a life is at stake prods me to telephone John and tell him that I have to see him.

The Leap _____

*J*ohn Sherrill . . . Tib and I were having coffee in bed this morning after a sleepless night when the telephone rang. It was our neighbor, Catherine LeSourd, asking Tib and me to come over right away. Catherine met us at the door dressed in a housecoat, wearing neither makeup nor smile, which said more than words about the concern she was feeling. She led us into the family room, shut the door, and without polite talk, began.

"First of all I want to say that I know this is presumptuous of me. I'm going to talk to you about your religious life, and I have no right to assume that it lacks anything. After all, you've been writing for *Guideposts* for almost ten years; you respect religion, you've studied it from many angles. But there is so much more to it than that.

"John," Catherine pressed on, "do you believe Jesus was God?"

It was the last question in the world I'd expected. I'd supposed she'd have something to say about God being able to heal, or prayer being the antidote to fear—something to do with tomorrow's surgery.

But she'd put the question to me, so I considered it. Tib and I were Christian, certainly, in the sense that we wrote "Protestant" on application blanks, attended church with some regularity, sent our three children to Sunday school. Still, I knew that these were habits; the fact was, I had never come to grips with this very question. Was Jesus of Nazareth, in fact, God? And now, when I tried, there were mountains of logic that halted me. I started to map them for Catherine, but she stopped me.

"You're trying to approach Christianity through your mind, John," she said. "It simply can't be done that way.

"It's one of the peculiarities of Christianity," she went on, "that you cannot come to it through intellect. You have to be willing to experience it first, to do something you don't understand—and then, oddly enough, understanding often follows. And it's just that which I'm hoping for you today, that without understanding, without even knowing why, you say yes to Christ."

There was silence in the room. I had an eternity of reservations—and less than a day before going to the operating table. The biggest reservation of all was precisely that: it just didn't seem right to shy away from wholehearted commitment all these years and then come running when I had cancer and was scared and had my back to the wall.

"I'd feel like a hypocrite," I said.

"John," said Catherine almost in a whisper, "that's pride. You want to come to God in your way. When you will. As you will. Strong and healthy. Maybe God wants you now, without a shred to recommend you."

We talked for perhaps half an hour more, and when we

left I still had not brought myself to make that step that was apparently all-crucial. In the car a few moments later, however, I turned to Tib. "What do they call it, 'a leap of faith'?" I said. "All right, I'm going to make the leap: I believe that Jesus was God."

It was a cold-blooded laying down of my sense of what was logical, quite without emotional conviction. And with it went something that was essentially "me." All the bundle of self-consciousness that we call our ego seemed somehow involved in this decision. It was amazing how much it hurt, how desperately this thing fought for life, so that there was a real kind of death involved. But when it was dead and quiet finally, and I blurted out my simple statement of belief, there was room in me for something new and altogether mysterious.

Len . . . At the time of his second cancer crisis, John and Tib were working on a book about modern-day manifestations of the Holy Spirit. They'd completed a first draft—very objective, very much a compilation of "other people's experiences"—when Catherine made that telephone call. In the intensely personal book the Sherrills ultimately produced, *They Speak with Other Tongues*, they describe what followed: a miraculous healing, a personal encounter with Jesus, eventually John's baptism in the Holy Spirit.

Our relationship with the Sherrills took on new dimensions, too, as the four of us began meeting weekly to share both family and work concerns. In Tib, Catherine found the sensitive editor she had long been seeking; soon her manuscript *Beyond Our Selves* was taking shape.

Catherine, fall 1961 . . . I'm full of joy and gratitude this morning, Lord. So much good is happening in our lives. A letter from Billy Graham yesterday is full of praise for my new book *Beyond Our Selves*. This praise belongs to You.

You give me the words, Lord. And the book is bringing people to You.

The editorial meetings at *Guideposts* are stimulating times. Yesterday we went over the two-part series John Sherrill is doing on David Wilkerson, who's done such amazing work with teenage gangs in New York City. I've never seen John so excited about a story.

John's recovery from his cancer operation is complete . . . his gratitude to You beautiful to behold.

To me the most remarkable event of 1961 is what has happened to Peter. Len and I have been praying so faithfully for Peter every morning—for almost two years now. And You have answered our prayers in the most spectacular way.

Last spring I was so discouraged. One evening Peter looked me straight in the eye and told me that when he graduated from college in June, he intended to be "a beach boy at Virginia Beach." I didn't believe him, of course, but he seemed so hostile to the Christian faith. It was Len who persuaded him to go to the conference at Estes Park, Colorado, put on by the Fellowship of Christian Athletes. You know the rest, Lord.

No More
Running Away _____

*P*eter John Marshall, fall 1961 ... If there was ever a lost soul, wandering about without purpose or direction, it was me in the summer of 1961. Having graduated from Yale University, I had come home to the red-shuttered house in Chappaqua with all my belongings—and no idea what to do next. I had no career plans (what does one do with a history degree if one doesn't want to teach?) and, to put it bluntly, no remote idea why I was living.

Up to this point, my life had been one of almost total self-centeredness, for I had withdrawn after my father's death into a world of lonely independence from everybody, including God. During my college years at Old Eli I had tried to fill the emptiness with the proverbial "wine, women, and song"; now in Chappaqua daily tennis matches were all that got me out of bed in the morning.

My stepfather, Len LeSourd, was on the board of the Fellowship of Christian Athletes, and he and my mother had to go to an FCA conference at Estes Park, Colorado, in July. Having nothing better to do, I went along for the fun of the athletics, but God had something else in mind.

The main speaker that week was Donn Moomaw, a huge former All-American center at UCLA. He was now a Presbyterian minister, and when he spoke to us young athletes about Jesus Christ being a man's man and the only man worth giving your life to, we listened.

Finally, toward the end of the conference, I waited until everyone else had left the large wooden auditorium, then went up to speak with Moomaw. I told him I had some questions about dating, but the Spirit of God enabled Donn to see through this smokescreen. "That's not what's the matter with you," he said. "Your problem is that you've been running away from God all your life. When are you going to be ready to give your life to Jesus Christ?"

Suddenly I had the strange sensation of standing about twenty feet away from myself, hearing myself say something I had no intention of saying. To my astonishment, what came out of me was: "Well, I guess I'm ready as I'll ever be."

Donn said, "That's the truth! Why don't you do it right now? Sit down and let's pray right here."

And we did. I knew what I was doing; my mother had always made it clear that giving your life to Christ meant giving up control, coming under His authority to live the rest of your life for His plans, not your own.

My prayer was short, even crude: "Lord, my life is a

mess. I have fouled it all up, and I'm sick of running it my way. You can have the whole stinking pile of garbage, and if You can do anything with it, it's all Yours."

During the next few days the sun of God's favor and love burned away the fog within like the hot Colorado sun dissolving the mountain mists. Now that I was seeking His will for my life, God moved with a speed that took my breath away.

After the conference, Mother, Len, and I flew to Los Angeles to visit Presbyterian minister Louis Evans and his wife, Colleen, whose house guest just happened to be the director of admissions at Princeton Theological Seminary. Praying for God's guidance about my future, I decided to talk to this man, and within days the Lord began opening doors. In August I was accepted for the September entering class at Princeton Seminary. Amazing—in that only a few weeks before all this, becoming a Christian, let alone a Christian minister, was the farthest thing from my mind!

And so now after years of avoiding God, I was following in my father's footsteps. What Jesus will do with my life, how He will lead me, remains to be seen. But at last I know that I am finally tracking with His loving plan for my life.

Explosion
of the Spirit _____

*C*atherine, spring 1962 ... This morning, Lord, Your power and Your joy and Your love seem to be trembling in the very air about me. First, the beautiful experience that happened to Len last night needs to be recorded here. He came to our prayer group last evening full of resentment against one of his associates. Several of us laid hands on him and prayed for a healing—specifically that he would be filled with the Holy Spirit. Nothing seemed to happen until. . . .

We'd gone to bed and I was dropping off when Len whispered, "Catherine, are you asleep?

"I have the strangest feeling," he went on. "There's this rushing, headlong joy inside me! It started in the pit of my stomach after I got in bed and now it's bubbling up right into my head. I can't control it. Catherine, I feel like praising God—on my knees!"

Both of us got up and knelt beside the bed.

Len's prayer began quietly enough. First he expressed gratitude for the friends who had prayed for him. Next he thanked God for our life together. After that he expressed love for each member of our family near and far. In between he kept telling the Lord how much he loved Him. Then heartfelt love rose from the depths of his being for the very individual who had been such a thorn in his side. Finally, he began God-blessing everyone he could think of, as if this love were so great it had to encompass the whole universe.

I was astonished. Always before Len's prayers had been short, even abrupt, well thought out, words carefully chosen, but quite unemotional. In contrast, words last night poured from him lavishly, exuberantly repetitious, a geyser of deep emotion unabashedly expressed. Like a bird uncaged, his emotions were darting, wheeling, soaring, wanting nothing so much as to keep flying forever.

Len's experience of the Spirit follows Peter's of last winter. Peter also was in a group—a small gathering of classmates at Princeton Seminary who prayed that Peter would receive the infilling. As with Len, Your coming, Lord, was precisely tailored to his need.

Peter, as a boy, suffered a lot of sadness—sadness that had been crammed deep down inside him. There was his bewilderment and loss as a small child when I was bedridden for almost three years, his enormous grief over the loss of his father at age nine. So when the Holy Spirit came into Peter, You produced laughter . . . laughter that welled up from the depths of his soul—up and up and up, never stopping for thirty minutes—a cleansing, healing flow washing the buried sorrow away. . . .

And still earlier came John Sherrill's remarkable experience. John's healing from cancer started a revolution in his life. What he discovered of the power of the Spirit in David Wilkerson intrigued John so much that this son of a liberal theologian decided to attend a convention on the Holy Spirit in Atlantic City.

What then took place in a hotel room was a kind of modern Damascus Road experience. First, Tib left the hotel to walk for miles along the seashore, deliberately taking with her the habitual reportorial onlooker's viewpoint. A group of half a dozen men then prayed for John to receive the Spirit. He told us later that the roof seemed to open up and light pour down on him. He found himself on the floor with his glasses spun off to one side, his notebook and pen to the other, and no idea how much time had gone by.

John phoned us in Chappaqua from Atlantic City an hour after he "came to." He was almost incoherent with excitement, saying over and over, "You've got to come down here. You've just got to come. Terrific things are going on."

We couldn't go down to Atlantic City then, but when John returned to Chappaqua several days later, he radiated the joy of the Spirit. Tib, too, although she had not had a personal experience, came back utterly persuaded of the reality of the things they had witnessed. A detective's daughter, Tib is suspicious of outward appearances. "Some of the excitement in the big meetings seemed worked-up," she told us. "And of course there were one or two exhibitionists. But I sat there in Atlantic City watching people experience God's love in a profound and life-transforming way."

With Len, Peter, and John—three of the most important people in my life—having such vivid encounters with You,

Lord, I have asked myself, "Am I missing something?" Going back through my life I realize that for a long time the term *Holy Spirit* was for me just a sort of religious garnish, a sprig of parsley on the ecclesiastical platter.

Then in the summer of 1944 as I lay bedridden from my lung ailment, a desire arose inside me to know more about this vague-seeming subject. This led me to months of topical Bible study on the Holy Spirit in both Old and New Testaments. What I discovered astonished me. My inescapable conclusion was that since Your resurrection, ascension, and glorification, and until You return again, we are living in the era of the Holy Spirit.

Without the Spirit we are without any vivid sense of Your presence. We are without guidance or wisdom or peace or joy or any effective witness to other people. And so very simply and very quietly, with no one else present, I asked for the gift of the Holy Spirit, accepted His coming into my life by faith, and began to live that out day by day.

Nothing overtly exciting happened. My experience was a completely solitary one. I didn't know anyone back then in the '40s who was walking this particular road. There was nothing being written about the Holy Spirit that I could find.

However, during the years that followed there have been many manifestations in my life. A new awareness of Your guidance, for example—the kind that cautions or confirms. Wisdom was available for small daily decisions. I didn't have to muddle through many situations as I had before, trying to figure out everything for myself. The Helper was right there.

The question I have this morning is, "Is there something more?" This love everyone speaks of—You know, Lord, how badly I need that right now! After two and a half years of being mother to this family, the home situation is no easier. Harder, in fact, as the children get older. Len and I can't seem to agree on discipline, bedtimes, homework hours—anything. With Linda, especially, we're constantly at loggerheads. Linda flouts my rules, and I display my insecurity by losing my temper.

A Christian home should be a haven of peace, Lord; ours is too often a battlefield. How I need the love that flows from You!

Conflict _____

*L*inda . . . So many emotions were churning around inside me when Dad remarried. At ten I thought I was pretty adult. But looking back, I realize I was in great need of someone who understood my confused thoughts and emotions and could have helped me sort them out.

Eve ("Mommy," as I called her then) had been a wonderful mother to me in my very early years. We had done everything together and she treated me as her chief confidante. In fact, that became a problem. The burden of sometimes buying her liquor and secretly helping her dispose of the bottles in brown paper bags weighed heavily on me.

During my mother's long absences I missed her terribly and desperately, prayed she'd get better so we could be a normal, happy family again. Did some well-meaning but misguided adult suggest I must look after my younger brothers? Certainly I felt I should. I remember myself at nine, playing the little mother, preparing orange juice and doughnuts to serve with Saturday morning cartoons. Poor caretaker that I was, I was better than some of the house-keepers. One beat me with a belt when Dad went away on a trip. (She was fired.) And it seemed we were always being shuttled around to grandparents' or friends' houses.

When Dad married Catherine ("Mom," as I soon called her), I was excited. It signaled a return to normalcy. And a best-selling author seemed so glamorous to me! I'd even have an older brother, her son, Peter, a tall, handsome, worldly-wise college sophomore.

Yet I often thought of my "real mommy." Once years before she had awakened me at night, desperate for reas-surance.

"Promise me one thing, Linda?"

"Sure, Mommy."

Her voice caught. "If you ever have another mother, promise me you won't call her 'Mommy.' Promise me I'll always be your 'Mommy.' "

I didn't know what she was talking about. "But Mommy, I don't *want* any other Mommy. I only want you. I want you to get well."

"Promise me, Linda?"

"I promise."

Thus began my difficulties with my stepmother, before I ever had one.

When Dad returned from his honeymoon with our new "Mom," they moved into a new house in a new community. Soon my brothers and I joined them—and right away I could see that things were not going to be as great as I had thought. As the new girl in my fifth-grade class I guess I tried too hard to show my classmates how great our family was: my dad an important editor ... my new mother a

famous writer . . . my big brother at Yale. It was too heady
for a ten-year-old to handle very well.

My stepmother and I soon began to clash over all sorts of
things: clothes, food, bedtime, money, duties around the
house. For someone who had had very little discipline up
to then, this super-structured new home life came as a
blow. To make things worse, I felt I had lost my father. When
he wasn't working in Manhattan, he and Mom were going
places, doing things, often without me and the boys. It
seemed that we saw more of the live-in housekeeper than
our parents.

Eventually I made it into the "in" crowd at school. That
entailed "hanging out" at local restaurants, weekend par-
ties, trying out alcohol and cigarettes. All of these things
were forbidden to me, and I chafed at being the most re-
stricted of the group. Occasionally I would sneak out of the
house to join my friends, or lock myself into the bathroom
to smoke. When Mom caught me at these things, there were
some pretty bad scenes. Even Dad was upset with me at
times, but usually he'd just leave the room and later I could
hear raised voices behind my parents' door.

My schoolwork was another battleground. Though I had
always been a straight A student, my grades now seesawed
wildly. Sadly, I think it was my way of "getting back" at my
parents; no doubt it was also a cry for help. And help I got—
a teacher from school was hired as my tutor. But I spent
more energy trying to outsmart him than in doing my assignments.

Mom was warm and nice to me when I followed the rules
at home and performed well in school. But I didn't feel she
understood me—or wanted to try. I knew Dad loved me, but
most of his time seemed to be spent smoothing over conflicts between Mom and me. I'd been his "Number One girl"
for so long—now I felt I'd lost him.

As I entered my teens I was a very unhappy girl.

Family Crisis _____

*L*en ... The early '60s were exciting times ... high creativity and productivity ... exploring the Holy Spirit phenomenon ... stimulating travel. Challenging times, too, as the strong personalities in our combined families frequently clashed. I was often the man-in-the-middle, trying to balance the legitimate demands, for example, of both my wife and my daughter. Trying to keep peace in the family.

In 1965 there was a wonderful new addition to that family. For years Catherine had been praying for her son's future mate. She had even written down a description of her: "Strong Christian, tall because Peter's so tall, probably blonde, fun to be with. . . ." Peter met Edith Wallis, a fellow student, at Princeton Theological Seminary during his final year there. Peter knew nothing about his mother's prayer and would probably have called it "spiritual manipulation" if he had. In any case he fell in love with Edith: tall, blonde, and definitely "fun to be with." They were married in 1965 and settled in West Hartford, Connecticut, where Peter became assistant pastor at a Presbyterian church.

On a trip to the Holy Land in the summer of 1963 Catherine had contracted a bad case of bronchitis. When it lingered on throughout the following winter, threatening a return of her dreaded lung ailment, doctors urged a move to a warmer climate. We bought a house in Florida in the spring of 1964 and moved to Boynton Beach that fall. Catherine's mother, Leonora Wood, joined us there in the cold months. For me it meant long-distance commuting to my job at *Guideposts*, alternating one week in New York and one week in Florida. I did this for ten years.

The close relationship with the Sherrills continued, with Tib making frequent trips to Boynton Beach as work progressed on Catherine's novel, *Christy*. Linda was now at Emma Willard School in Troy, New York, while Chet and Jeff attended Florida schools. Physical separation eased the tension between Catherine and Linda, but I sensed that basic issues remained unresolved.

Meanwhile the relationship between Catherine and me was suffering. From comments she let drop almost without being aware of them, I could tell that she had never really come to terms with the fact of my divorce. The grinding back-and-forth commute I had from Florida to New York did not make for family closeness either. And then came a family emergency.

Catherine, November 27, 1966 ... Lord, because I know You sometimes communicate with us in dreams, I cannot stop thinking about the terrifying one Mother had last week. It was about the baby Edith is carrying, due any day now. Mother dreamed that the baby was in a basket on a little boat in a rushing stream. One end of a fragile cord was attached to the boat. The other end was in Mother's hands and she was struggling to bring the boat onto shore.

Then the stream disappeared out of the dream, and Mother was standing in front of a stoop behind which was a narrow door, holding the basket in her hands. As she laid the basket down to open the door, all at once the baby disappeared from the basket.

Mother woke, shaking.

Lord, was this just an ordinary nightmare—or was it from You? And if so, what does this mean?

December 3, 1966 ... Two weeks after Mother's dream Edith had her baby. Peter called to say it was a boy, but his voice was not as excited as a man's should be over his first child. Then it came. "Something's wrong, Mom. 'Poor muscle tone,' the doctors call it."

Lung congestion followed, the threat of pneumonia. On Sunday Peter crawled in under the oxygen tent to christen the baby Peter Christopher—"Christ-bearer."

All who saw Peter Christopher sensed something unusual within the perfectly formed little body, the round head covered with just a hint of blonde fuzz. People used the word *gentle* when they spoke of him—"a beautiful gentle spirit."

A torrent of prayer went up for Peter Christopher Marshall.

Edith ... Mom arrived at the Hartford Hospital from Florida on December 17. She had wanted very much to come earlier, but had felt restrained by the Holy Spirit—for what reason she did not know. I remember it was a very cold day and she was bundled up in a heavy coat. Entering Peter Christopher's room in the pediatric ward, she first hugged Peter and me, then headed to the little crib where the baby was sleeping underneath an oxygen tent.

She caressed his little body, touched his head, and commented on how beautiful he was. Then, after a few preliminary words to Peter and me, explaining that the Holy Spirit had given her this directive, she reached under the tent, and laying both hands on little Peter, she said a prayer which I recognized as essentially one of relinquishment. She concluded with these words:

"Peter Christopher, you are His little prince, and as such I am authorized and directed to crown you with thanksgiving." I sensed in her voice that with this prayer she had fulfilled some kind of responsibility.

Shortly thereafter a nurse, checking underneath the oxygen tent, noticed that the baby was in distress. The three of us (Peter, Mom, and I) were asked to leave the room while a red-headed intern did an examination. A few minutes later, the doctor came out and told us in the hallway that Peter Christopher had died.

For a while we were all too stricken to speak. What Mom said at last was: "I got here in time to do what I was commissioned to do."

Peter . . . Edith and I decided that the funeral service for Peter Christopher had to express victory. As I stood in the pulpit, looking down at the tiny white casket, only 36 inches long, I spelled out the truth from Scripture as I believed it:

> For I am persuaded that neither death nor life . . . shall be able to separate us from the love of God.
>
> Romans 8:38–39, NKJ

> In all these things we are more than conquerors through him who loved us.
>
> Romans 8:37, NKJ

> Glory in this . . . that I am the Lord, exercising lovingkindness, judgment, and righteousness in the earth.
>
> Jeremiah 9:24, NKJ

Then I explained that Edith and I were comforted by the knowledge that even though we couldn't understand why the Lord had allowed such a thing to happen to our first-born, nevertheless He was still a God who could be trusted.

"A deeper understanding of the meaning of life is ours because of our experience with Peter Christopher," I went on, speaking for us both. "For life is not to be measured in length of days, but rather in how well we fulfill our destiny. We believe that in two short weeks Peter Christopher has perfectly fulfilled his destiny and his purpose."

Len ... The loss of her grandson was a severe blow to Catherine, but her grief was normal and not prolonged. The deaths of both her first husband (in 1949) and her father (in 1961) had prepared her to face and accept sudden loss. Moreover, the special commission to Peter Christopher given her by the Holy Spirit reassured her, and Peter and Edith, that the baby's future was truly in God's hands. For this, our whole family gave thanksgiving.

Furthermore, Peter and Edith would be having more children.

Taking Correction _____

*C*atherine, *spring 1967* ... Lord, I come to You each morning for a time of fellowship together ... to share my concerns, to feel Your love, to receive Your guidance and, yes, even Your reproof.

Len and I had a heated session the other night during which he spoke words of correction to me about my tendency to be critical, my aloofness from people, my inability to demonstrate love even to certain members of my own family. I knew there was truth in what he said and he did it lovingly, but I was resistant.

After that session with Len, it was obvious to me that

revelations that come from the inside, from You, Lord, I can "take" with ease—no matter how negative they may be.

Whereas if the same insights come from another human being, they are immediately suspect and get me wrought up. I confess this as stubbornness on my part and I see it as building a barrier between Len and me.

Jesus, I hear You speak even as I write these words on paper. Len, as my husband, is the spiritual head of our home. He has the right, even the responsibility, to correct the members of his family. I need to see You in Len and trust that You are working in him.

But I confess something else here, Lord. I continue to be troubled in my spirit about Len's divorce. I thought I heard Your will on this before I married him. There has been no problem with his first wife. Not only is there no bitterness between them, there is gratitude on her part for Len's financial support. And she hasn't asked for visitation rights to the children during the seven-plus years Len and I have been married.

Perhaps the real reason for my uneasiness is the question I keep asking myself: "Did I have a right to remarry? Was that in any way a betrayal of Peter?"

Perhaps I only kidded and rationalized myself into thinking that I *did* have Your approval to remarry. Could the truth have been for me that I was meant to be content in the state in which I found myself after Peter's death?

After You Yourself had opened the door into the writing world for me, and authored my books and blessed them immeasurably, did You not mean for me to be grateful and to leave it there?

In marrying Len, was I not manipulating? Was it man-made, not God-given? Was it the result of my rebelling against the single condition to which You had called me, thereby violating a law of the Spirit?

So now—I open myself to Your mercy, Lord. You alone can help me through this situation.

Summer 1967 ... During the years of my widowhood I dreamed periodically that Peter Marshall was not dead, but was waiting somewhere for me. Last night I had this same dream.

Peter appeared to be in some sort of institution where there were lots of people and where he had some sort of position. With a thrill of recognition I spotted him: he was dancing! At last his eyes met mine. He seemed greatly surprised (I had already noted that there was no ring on his left hand).

He stopped dancing, came over to me, and began talking. Here I cannot recapture all the dream, only that Peter shook my hand rather than kissing me. He was friendly and open, but not a lover. In the dream both he and I knew that I had married again.

The dream might have been prompted by a counseling session I had a few days ago with a woman separated from her husband. I was pretty blunt in warning her about the price both husband and wife pay if they divorce, all the while resurrecting, I fear, the guilt I feel in marrying a divorced man.

Fall 1967 ... A Bible verse is alive for me this morning, Lord. "Come out from among them and be ye separate" (2 Corinthians 6:17, KJV).

You call for a "peculiar people." Nudged by this word I did a quick personal inventory. Yes, I'm certainly one of those peculiar ones who never went along with "the crowd." In fact, if "the crowd" was for something, then I was usually against it.

There was that weekend at college when the gang wanted to stay up all night. I thought this was silly, so was the only one who went to bed. In a sense this was rebellion—and rebellion is seldom right.

I was so resistant to peer pressure that I never won an elective school office in my life. I told myself that I didn't care, but of course, I did care.

This determination to be "different" undoubtedly came from my parents who cherished me so intensely that they convinced me that I was of finer clay than ordinary humanity, destined for great things.

I see on reflection this morning that this "finer clay" philosophy can be a highly dangerous one. What can it lead to except pride, self-centeredness, even arrogance? Scripture instructs us not to think of ourselves more highly than we ought. Is "being different" not a denial of my common humanity?

I do not want to displease You, Lord. I want to be different, peculiar, for You.

Summer 1968 . . . How can I show my gratitude, Lord, for the success of my novel, *Christy*? It has been up to number two on the *New York Times* bestseller list, been picked up by the *Reader's Digest* book club, and a motion picture sale is in the works. It was over nine years ago when I started work on *Christy*, wondering if I *could* write a novel. Thank You, Lord, for giving me the ideas, the persistence, and the editorial help to bring it off.

Edith Marshall, March 1, 1969 . . . As I lay in the delivery room at Goddard Memorial Hospital in Stoughton, Massachusetts, I had no thought but that we were going to have a bouncing, healthy baby. The doctors had given us no reason to suspect otherwise. Having done our grief work, the pain of Peter Christopher's death had been put behind us, and we were filled with the anticipation of child-rearing.

Peter was pastoring his own church now on Cape Cod, the East Dennis Community Church. .

We had traveled seventy miles from our home on Cape Cod to find a doctor who was supportive of our desire to be active participants in the birth process through "natural childbirth." Goddard Hospital where he worked welcomed prepared fathers into the labor room—though not yet, in those days, into the actual delivery room. We wanted to give our baby the best possible start in life: a birth free from the effects of anesthesia and two eager and attuned parents ready to welcome and bond with their baby immediately after birth. We were excited.

And we were not disappointed. Mary Elizabeth was born amidst jubilant whoops. My exhilaration was overwhelming. She couldn't have been healthier, more beautiful, more loved. The joy of motherhood was mine at last.

Peter Marshall ... As I helped Edith through her labor, I was the typical anxious father. After they wheeled her into delivery the waiting seemed eternal, while I paced around the little area for fathers out in the hospital corridor. Finally, the delivery room nurse came out to tell me that we had a baby girl. My heart leapt inside me—a moment of pure, unalloyed joy!

But our loving and gracious God had still more for us. While the doctor and nurses were finishing up with Edith, one of the pediatric nurses came out into the hall to speak to me.

"Mr. Marshall, I have been a pediatric nurse for twenty-five years, and I want to tell you something. In all my years of caring for newborns, I have never seen a baby with such perfect muscle tone!"

Perfect muscle tone—the precise thing that Peter Christopher lacked. The nurse knew nothing of our previous infant, of course, yet the Lord used her to speak the words He knew would reassure me most.

Gloria _____

*C*atherine, spring 1969 . . . My search for my next major book project is over. It will be a novel . . . based on the life of a remarkable woman who lives here in south Florida. I will call her Gloria. In fact, *Gloria* would make a good title for the book.

I have been off-and-on about this project for months. Yet ever since meeting her I knew intuitively that I had a jewel in Gloria's story, although admittedly an uncut one. Others who know her, Tib Sherrill, members of my family, have not appreciated the gem, doubted that it was worth a book setting, suspected even that it might be fake.

But something inside has made me hang on. I've listened to the doubters, I've doubted myself sometimes, wondering if her far-out experiences are authentic. How can I be sure? For Jesus' sake, I cannot, dare not pass along anything to my readers that is not 100 percent genuine.

Evelyn Underhill's book *Mysticism* has impressed me. It tells me that (1) in Gloria I have on my hands a modern mystic; and (2) that there is a solid philosophical and psychological base for mysticism. So far, so good. Then comes my personal counterreaction. It goes like this: But what good will it do to write a book for general consumption on such a specialized example of mysticism as Gloria? Aren't the mystics, like the prophets, especially singled out and endowed people?

I am torn here between wanting to write a book that will have a broad common denominator, and one that will have much of the supernatural in it. I sense that they pay a heavy price who have supernatural gifts. So what can a book like *Gloria* have for the average reader today? Why not just spin a good story and let it go at that?

Now this morning an insight from God's Word: "And it shall come to pass in the last days, saith God, I will pour out of my Spirit upon *all flesh:* and your sons and your daughters shall prophesy, your young men shall see visions and your old men shall dream dreams" (Acts 2:17, NJV).

The question is, have we arrived at the time for this prophecy to be fulfilled? Can the hippie movement be evidence that the last days are upon us? Maybe the young in their restless search for "something beyond" are really hungering for the fulfillment of Joel's prophecy.

Perhaps the charismatic renewal is part of this, too. Sure, the wheat here has to be separated from the chaff. But let us not be misled by the chaff into thinking that there are no kernels of wheat.

So what does all this mean regarding *Gloria?*

That I am to trust my instincts here. Yes, Gloria has some silly foibles and goes off on tangents. But so did many of the saints.

My conclusion: I am to go full speed ahead with *Gloria*. Since I don't see *how* to write it, God will show me how. It's as simple and as magnificent as that.

Summer 1969 . . . I had this curious dream about Tib Sherrill. Something was wrong with her so that she had to make the decision to allow surgeons to cut off both her legs to save her life. She wept. I wept. In the dream I went through a period of rebellion for her. How *could* she make such an irreversible decision?

But she made it and the night came when she had to prepare to enter the hospital for the dreadful operation.

I went through agony and an emotional upheaval—and there the dream ended.

What is the correct interpretation of this dream? Is there a message in it—something I'm supposed to convey to Tib?

When I took it to my prayer group, one woman felt that the dream was not about Tib at all, but about me. I was the one about to lose my legs, meaning that I was about to go through the rest of my life maimed, a cripple, only half a person.

Is my subconscious trying to tell me through this dream that my household situation and marriage have made me half a person, that they are beginning to cripple my creativity?

Another possible interpretation—Tib Sherrill represents a portion of my own being. Probably the writer part. Perhaps even more specifically, the new book I'm working on, *Gloria*.

For many years Tib worked with me on *Christy*. I counted on her input so heavily that even during the year she and John and their children spent in Bolivia, chapters were constantly in the mail between Florida and South America. Now Tib does not feel she can be part of the *Gloria* project.

Therefore, one possible interpretation of the dream is that

I have been depending too much upon editorial help, using it as a crutch, and that my subconscious mind is terrified at the idea of going ahead without it. Perhaps the real problem in my subconscious is that I am grieving over Tib's unwillingness to see the potential in *Gloria*. Len has always been lukewarm to this book—and anyhow Len is too involved at *Guideposts* to give me the help I need.

I know that there was fear in the dream and that the fear probably has to do with my writing. So I can begin praying at that point anyway.

God *could* be asking me via the dream, "Are you *willing* to have Me remove all human props from your writing and rely only on Me?"

Tib . . . I knew ahead of time that the editorial session on *Gloria* would be fiery.

Critiquing Catherine's writing was always hard because she identified so personally with her work. Fans of hers would often comment wistfully to me on my good fortune in knowing "the real Catherine." And to know her *was* good. For friends of Catherine, life was never dull. Her integrity, her high standards, her impatience with spiritual fence-sitting, made her friendship worth more than that of a dozen comfortable, undemanding souls.

But there was a part of Catherine that I felt was often concealed in face-to-face contact, even from intimates. This fear of exposure, this tendency to "run up the back stairs," in her own phrase, was to change in the early 1970s. Her time of darkness was to bring about this and other transformations.

But from the beginning, Catherine had no hesitancy in putting herself, all of herself, onto paper. Her readers—I among them—knew a "real Catherine" who might otherwise have stayed hidden. Her warmth, her vulnerability, her intense caring, flowed from her pen like the life blood that, in truth, it was for her.

I never had to ask Catherine how a morning's work had gone; her face across the lunch table told me exactly how many pages she'd written and how good or bad she thought they were. Suggesting changes in work so inextricably tied up with her very self was always an ordeal—both for me to make and for her to hear. All writers, no matter how bright the smile we glue to our lips, die a little when told we must redo something. We call a manuscript *it*, but it's really *us* and it hurts like surgery to reshape it.

With Catherine this universal writer's reaction was intensified. Catherine had no plastic smile to paste on at such moments; her face betrayed everything she felt. I think this is one reason person-to-person encounters were so threatening to her—the bland social cover-up was no part of her armory. Getting a negative reaction to the morning's work, her face would blanch as from a physical blow. Often she'd escape to some solitary corner of whatever house, hers or mine, we were working in, taking the imperiled pages with her as one would snatch a child from an attacker.

Soon, however, she'd be back, manuscript in hand. "What else is wrong?"

Her commitment to excellence made her pursue criticism, in spite of the pain, from Len, from me, from her publishers.

With *Gloria*, however, I knew the pain would be fiercer than usual. In spite of initial unenthusiastic responses from both Len and me, she'd invested months in interviewing, additional months in writing. She'd sent me an outline and a draft of the early chapters and was waiting now for my reaction.

The meeting took place at a country inn in New Hampshire where she and Len had gone for a brief holiday. John and I drove up one August day with the idea that Catherine and I would have an initial session on the book that afternoon, after which the four of us would have dinner.

That night nobody ate. At six o'clock John and Len ar-

rived at the room where Catherine and I were working, to
find her pacing the narrow space between the beds.

"You're telling me I'm not capable of getting a complex
personality on paper!"

"I'm saying that Gloria sends mixed messages. And that a
fiction writer has to find some unifying principle in his
principal character. Real life doesn't have to be consistent.
Fiction does."

"And you think I'm not capable of doing that."

"Of course you're capable. What I'm asking is, should
you? Does this project have your name on it—or is it a
distraction? A temptation, even, pulling you away from the
book God has for you?"

"God told me to write about Gloria."

"Then do. Write about her. Write about the impact she's
had on you. On Catherine. It's trying to write as Gloria that I
question. To write in first person you have to feel some
identity with your subject. Let me ask you bluntly, Catherine: do you like Gloria?"

Catherine stopped her agitated pacing to stare through
the window at the peaks of the White Mountains on fire in
the setting sun. "She baffles me," Catherine admitted. "But I
certainly don't agree with what you write here—" She
ruffled through the pages in her hands. "Where you say
she's crazy."

"I didn't say crazy. I said emotionally unstable."

"It's the same thing."

"It's not the same thing. Rational people can have irra-
tional areas."

"All right," Catherine said, "your term was unstable.
And yet you say here—" she pulled out another page "—
that you want the vision scene to show 'her genuine spirituality.' Which is it? Is she an authentic mystic, or a very
mixed-up woman?"

"I think she's both, Catherine. And I don't think you'll
ever be comfortable with those contradictions in her."

"Well, can you explain to me why God would lavish such tremendous spiritual gifts on a woman who's as kooky as you seem to think?"

"No. Indeed I can't explain it. But because I don't understand something doesn't mean it isn't so."

And so it went, as the shadows traveled up the mountain slopes beyond the window, with John from time to time forlornly suggesting dinner and Len trying to keep the peace between two opinionated women. The only thing the New Hampshire trip decided was that Catherine would continue, alone, with the writing of *Gloria*.

Len . . . I had some serious reservations as to whether or not Catherine should do the *Gloria* book, but these had less to do with Gloria herself and more to do with whether or not Catherine could handle this type of material, especially Gloria's promiscuous teen years. Tib Sherrill felt that Catherine's lack of sympathy for the adolescent Gloria would make those episodes unconvincing. A McGraw-Hill editor was partly responsible for Catherine's absorption with Gloria's seamy past. He told us, "Catherine Marshall writing sex scenes. That will sure get the public's attention!" Maybe. Maybe not.

To me Gloria's conversion and walk with Jesus seemed the most promising area. Gloria not only hears the voice of Jesus, but according to her own report, sees into the heavenly kingdom. I remember one day in particular. . . .

I had just returned to our Florida home from New York City. When I arrived home Catherine and Gloria were in the living room. The three of us chatted for a while and then I disclosed a problem situation at the office that was bothering me.

"Let's pray about it, Len," Catherine suggested. "Maybe we should lay hands on you."

I was willing and sat down in the chair facing the window. At that moment Catherine was called to the telephone.

She asked Gloria to go ahead and pray without her. Gloria stood behind me silently for a moment. I waited. Nothing happened. Instead Gloria picked up her purse, walked out the front door, got into her car, and drove off.

Somewhat nonplused, I took my bag to the bedroom and started unpacking. Catherine joined me a few minutes later.

"Where's Gloria?" she asked. "Did she pray for you?"

"No. She just walked out the door and drove off."

"How strange."

Ten minutes later I answered the phone. It was Gloria. "I'm sure you're wondering why I left when I did," she said.

"Well—yes."

"There was no need for me to pray," she said. "Two angels were already there praying for you, one on each side of the chair, kneeling by your side. I felt I should leave."

Stunned, I hardly knew what to say. Could it really be true? I believed in the existence of angels, but did they really have human-like shapes that could be discerned by certain people? And were they that involved with the workaday concerns of our lives?

Amazingly, the office problem was resolved by the time I flew back to New York. The whole episode haunted me for days, weeks—and helped me understand the fascination Gloria held for Catherine.

The Generation Gap _____

*C*atherine, *January 2, 1970* . . . Night before last the New Year was ushered in with the "Episode of the Chair." Len and I were flattered and delighted when Chester, 17, and Jeff, 14, elected to spend New Year's Eve at home playing bridge, just the four of us. Jeff was my partner, sitting opposite me in the mahogany, velvet-seated armchair, an antique that I especially prized. He and I lost the game, Jeff going down with a hand he should have made. In a burst of overdramatic frustration, he banged his hand on the table and sprang to his feet, knocking the chair backward. One arm of the chair was broken in two pieces.

Upset, I stormed at Jeff that all his privileges would be taken away for the weekend.

Len, in turn, became angry at me in front of Jeff and
Chester, saying, "This kind of punishment has to be decided *between* us apart from the boys."

We were all tired, all edgy. Household harmony had already been stretched to the breaking point by too many
guests, too much activity over the holidays. When we went
to bed that night, Len and I were scarcely speaking.

The next day, yesterday, our relationship was still
strained when Len announced that two of his friends
from Ohio Wesleyan were "dropping by," a Methodist
preacher and his wife. I was less than enthusiastic at
the news.

In our living room, however, the preacher told a story that
has lingered with me. A friend of his lost a small child
through illness. He was bitter that his prayers for healing
had not been answered.

He told of the preacher going out into the starry night,
realizing that he had but two courses: he could go on railing
against God, hating God, and thus become estranged from
Him.

Or, he could obey St. Paul's injunction, "In everything,
give thanks," and praise God—even thought he didn't understand *why* God had let his child die, even though his
praise would be mechanical and halting.

He chose the latter course and started in, "Thank You,
God, for giving us such a beautiful child and for letting us
have the joy of her for two years." The man reported to the
preacher that *from the minute* he began this mechanical
praise, a tremendous weight lifted from his soul and he
began to see the face of his God again.

I thought about our loss of Peter Christopher and how our
thanksgiving had lifted us out of the pit then. It came to
me that the only way I could live with my present situation
and keep my sanity was to actually find *something* in
Jeff's outbursts, in Len's permissiveness with both

boys, in a hundred things in our household, *to praise God for.*

So now I ask, "But how can I thank You, Lord, for situations brought about by human failure and sin?" My own included.

I hear You telling me to reread the story of Joseph being sold into slavery—certainly the result of sin in his brothers. But as Joseph examined himself during those years in prison in Egypt, he no doubt came up with the realization that sin in himself—arrogance, judging, bragging—had helped produce the sin in his brothers. So everyone involved had sinned. Yet Joseph found cause to praise God.

It would appear that praise is the only way, Lord. Even with all our mistakes, You have still "allowed" us to make them. Thus we are still under Your permissive will. Help me, therefore, to praise You in *every circumstance.*

Len, May 1970 . . . "Be firm now," I told myself as I drove to Stuyvesant Hall on the Ohio Wesleyan campus where our daughter, Linda, was now a junior. It was parents' weekend and I had flown up from Florida. An engagement kept Catherine from joining me, but before I left, she and I had agreed that we were not going to underwrite college expenses if Linda continued spending her time in peace marches and protest meetings.

This was shortly after the four Kent State, Ohio, students had been killed by the National Guard. At nearby Ohio Wesleyan the ROTC building had been taken over for a day in protest, the administration building partly occupied, classes suspended for two days. Linda had been peripherally involved in all this.

I remembered the past Christmas when Linda had given a talk from the pulpit of our church on her summer experience in a ministry to inner-city children in San Diego,

California. An offshoot of the ministry of our friends Louis and Colleen Evans, this program seemed to have deeply affected Linda. She came back talking about racial prejudice, poverty, involvement, sensitivity. I'd been proud of her then—but these student activities against the war were something else.

I hoped for a relaxed lunch with Linda, during which we could come to some sensible conclusions about the importance of education as against marches and demonstrations. Linda greeted me with a question: "Would you like to see what's going on here? Lunch can wait, can't it?"

Stomach grumbling, I drove her in my rented car to Gray Chapel. "By the way, Dad," she said, "I didn't tell you and Mom something the other night on the phone. Five of us from Wesleyan went to Washington, D.C., for the march at the Capitol. The Transcript [the college paper] paid my expenses."

"Why didn't you tell us on the phone?"

"Well, you both seemed so uptight about everything."

While digesting this piece of news, my mind went back fifteen years to the little girl who liked to jump on my lap and throw her arms around my neck. In many ways I hardly knew this twenty-year-old with the granny glasses, long black hair, jeans, sandals.

We parked the car and joined some 500 students heading for the Chapel, the main assembly hall on campus. Much in evidence were long hair, dungarees, open shirts, bare feet.

Thirty years before when I was a student on this same campus, we wore saddle shoes, loud socks, sports coats, Joe College hats. Nothing had changed really; conformity was still the rule.

But what the students were doing was definitely different! Mimeographed literature was being passed out: statistics on the Vietnam War, on taxes, on the draft. The students then split into small groups to plan local action. Thirty years ago in May, I recalled, our big spring demonstration was a "panty raid" on the freshman girls' dormitory.

Linda and I walked across the campus to the recreation center, joining a group discussing a student plan to visit homes in the community. A girl with long, copper-hued hair was speaking.

"When you knock on a door," she was saying, "be friendly, be courteous, and for crying out loud, be neat."

"You mean we have to cut our hair?"

"Yes. Guys with long hair might just as well not go. Another point—let them talk. We want to get across our conviction about stopping the war, sure. But we also want to win friends. If the adults want to talk about campus violence, settle for that and let them know we're against this, too."

The girl read a summary of the instructions from a mimeographed sheet: "Communicate . . . talk, not tell . . . conversation with love."

I asked Linda if I could have a copy and she got one for me. We next visited a group discussing a proposed student boycott of Coca-Cola.

"Why pick a company that isn't making war materials?" someone asked.

The leader explained that students had to show their economic power in some way. They couldn't boycott General Motors cars with any effectiveness, but they could stop buying Coca Cola. The ultimate aim: have the Coca-Cola directors make a statement against the war.

I looked at Linda. "You're on shaky ground with this project." She nodded.

As we drove back to her dorm, I quizzed Linda about her trip to Washington. "I'm glad I went," she said. "It was an awesome experience and peaceful. We stumbled onto an SDS [Students for a Democratic Society] street meeting there. It was so far out it was ludicrous. We don't want to destroy America, we want to save it."

She paused for a moment. "Dad, I've been thinking about a lot more than politics. It began last summer when I woke up to the fact that the world is full of people who don't have the opportunities I've always taken for granted. I saw that I'd been living just for myself, and pretty superficially at that. Now I want to make a *difference* in the world.

"You and Mom have always talked about the importance of living out your faith. That's what I'm trying to do. I lead the high school group at William Street Church, I've been tutoring a sixth-grader, and I help plan the chapel 'Happenings' on campus. All this has meant more to me than the prayer group I attended for a while in the fall. I want to live for something bigger than myself, but I don't want to be tied down by religious labels."

Four hours had passed. Catherine might not care too much for Linda's social gospel approach, but I felt reassured by my daughter's idealism. Though I doubted that the Lord was first in her life, I sensed He had His hand on her. Now it was time for me to head for the airport.

Linda started to get out of the car, paused. "I hope you're not unhappy with me."

There it was. The little girl I remembered . . . uncertain . . . wanting love, reassurance. I reached out my hand and touched her cheek. It happened in a matter of seconds: generation gap, communication gap, parent-child gap all dissolved.

I drove to the airport feeling warmed inside. There's more to education, I decided, than books and classes.

Catherine, March 1971 . . . I had a dream last night that I should try to record. The exterior situation is that my sister and her family (with two teenage girls) arrived yesterday. Since Linda, Chester, and Jeff were all at home on spring vacations, that made five young people at the dinner table. I don't think that I've ever been so aware of the "generation gap." I felt as though we older ones were standing on the opposite bank of a great chasm.

In the dream, some people came into the bedroom where I was sleeping and forcibly kidnapped me. There were both males and females, obviously enemies who meant no good to me.

At one point, I remember being put on an operating table where a man shot something at me that hit my face. Immediately I knew that this would make me lose consciousness, and it did.

Len seemed to be somewhere on the edges of all this activity, by no means under the kind of assault I was, but also apparently a captive and unable to help me.

I can "get" no more of the dream except that the kidnapping seems to have arisen out of some statement I had made in a speech that did not please my enemies. Does the dream indicate I have an "adversary role" with teenagers? What am I to learn from this?

May 1971 ... Lord, this morning I'm in awe once more at what You've done. The report came from Chester who called last night all excited. He had gone from Taylor University in Upland, Indiana, where he is a sophomore, to a conference hosted by Roman Catholic charismatics at Notre Dame. Some 40,000 people had poured into South Bend, Indiana, nearly filling the Notre Dame stadium. Chester said he had never seen anything so powerful in all his life as 40,000 people on their feet, shouting and singing and praising the Lord.

What awes me is this. An article by one of the Catholic leaders attributes the origins of this Catholic renewal to three books: *The Cross and the Switchblade* by David Wilkerson (written by the Sherrills), *They Speak with Other Tongues* by John Sherrill, and *Nine O'Clock in the Morning* by Dennis Bennett.

Lord, memories flood back of that spring morning in 1960 when You prodded me into that confrontation with John Sherrill. What if I hadn't obeyed?

Obedience . . . obedience . . . obedience. How You depend upon it from Your children! How many great events should have happened but didn't because someone was not obedient! Scary to think about!

Husband/Wife Confrontation _____

*L*en, May 1971 ... After six years of commuting every other week from Florida to New York City, I felt quite literally split in two. Even members of my family were never quite sure where I was. Happily, *Guideposts* was doing well; in fact, becoming a major force in magazine publishing.

My major concern was the growing tension between Catherine and me. It was frustrating to come home after an exhausting week in New York only to be met with a new set of problems. Sometimes Catherine would start in as I was unpacking my bag:

"Jeff missed his school bus this morning. He overslept

because he stayed up late last night studying for a test. I had to drive him to school." (Jeff was then fifteen.)

"How did he do on the test?" I asked.

"He wouldn't tell me. I suspect he failed. Why don't you ask him?"

"I'll ask him tomorrow."

"If he did fail, I think he should be punished. Maybe no tennis this weekend."

I groaned. Tennis over the weekend was what Jeff and I most enjoyed doing together.

"If Jeff failed his test because he waited too late to study for it, he should be punished, I agree. But I'm not sure that depriving him of tennis is the answer."

"You'll let him off too easily."

I struggled to hide my annoyance. "At least give me a chance to unpack."

"You and I have never agreed on punishments for the children," Catherine persisted.

"I tend to be too easy on them, I admit it. But they're good kids. The boys have never given us trouble. You'll agree with that, won't you?"

"True," Catherine admitted. "Why do you think it's worked out that way?"

I had no trouble with that one. "Because we've prayed for them every day. And the structured home you set up for them when they were small. They thrived on this routine. I'll be eternally grateful to you for this, Catherine."

Catherine softened for a moment. "Then please don't resist me when I ask you to discipline them."

"The only time I resist is when I think you're being unloving."

"Like with Linda?" The edge was back in her voice.

"Well, yes."

"I wasn't really prepared to take on three small children when I married you."

We were back on rocky terrain. Familiar ground, especially in recent years. "Why do you keep bringing this up?"

"Because it's constantly on my mind. I feel that I'm living outside of God's will."

"You certainly didn't feel that way the first ten years of our marriage."

"At times I did. The pace of our lives back then was so fast I just didn't dwell on it."

"What you're saying, Catherine, is that when things were going well for you, you felt you were in God's will. Now that your book *Gloria* is not going well, and you have some relationship problems inside and outside the family, then you're out of God's will. And so you place the blame on the fact that you married a divorced man."

"It goes much deeper than that," Catherine replied. "I thought I'd heard God on the matter of your divorce before you and I were married. The unrest in my spirit began about five years ago. It came from—well I'm not sure just where."

"How about the women you meet with here in Florida?"

"The unrest began inside me first. I took it to them for prayer."

"And what came out of this prayer?"

Catherine was silent for a long moment. "I'm not quite sure. That possibly I was to have remained content in my single status."

I struggled with a growing irritation that I knew I had to keep under control. "All right, Catherine, you and your women prayer partners have come to the conclusion that possibly our marriage was not of God. What does this add up to now—today? Certainly not another divorce. Separation? How would that go down with your readers? We're really between a rock and a hard place, aren't we?"

Catherine nodded. "What you're saying is that I have to work this out between God and me."

"What I'm saying is, look at the positive accomplish-
ments you and I have achieved together over the past twelve
years. Shall I list them?"

"That's not necessary. I agree there are many."

"Then why would God bless our marriage so much if we
are out of His will?"

Catherine shook her head. "I'm sure lots of people who
are 'way out of God's will are accomplishing things that
appear to be blessed. That has nothing to do with the feeling of unrest I have about our marriage. It's troubled me for
years."

"Then let's go a different direction," I suggested. "Who
would benefit most from a rupture in our relationship?
Why don't you and your prayer partners come against the
dark powers that would love to do us in?"

"We have come against all dark forces, Len. These women are not your enemies. They want the best for us, they
want a healing here."

"What kind of healing?"

"We're not sure." Catherine took a deep breath. "You're
always saying that my attitudes need to change. I agree and
I'm trying. The question I have for you, Len, is: What about
your attitudes? What do you need to change?"

"About our marriage?"

"Well, yes. But I was thinking more about your divorce."

"I don't understand. A divorce is a divorce. What can you
change about that?"

"You can't change the fact of a divorce, but you can
change your attitude about it."

Taken by surprise, I struggled to put my thoughts together. "Divorce is always a tragedy. It's a terrible failure.
But for some marriages, it seems to be the only answer. I
tried for years to save my first marriage. Nothing seemed to
help. The divorce and remarriage gave my children a
chance for a stable home, a normal childhood. For me . . .
well, it freed me to find the creative life God had for me."

"Len, you're not really sure of that. God's perfect plan for you might have been to stick with the marriage, in spite of Eve's alcoholism, to work out a productive balance that could have had positive results beyond your wildest dreams."

I stared at Catherine in amazement ... speechless for a long stretch as I got very busy sorting some papers. Deep down I had to admit Catherine had scored a point. And I realized something else. Though unsettling, there was also something deeply fulfilling in these confrontations with Catherine. How I loved to watch her mental processes in action. How I loved her. Period.

"So how do I go about changing?" I finally asked.

"That's between you and the Lord," she replied.

I didn't sleep too well that night.

Dark Threads _____

Catherine, June 1971 ... Lord, everything in my world seems to be going awry. I'm at odds with the people closest to me. All my projects are stalled. Everything seems to be out of sync except my relationship with You:

(1) The movie of *Christy*. MGM paid a lot of money for this, hired a writer at great expense to do the script, shot a lot of footage in the Great Smoky Mountains. Now it's all been shelved.

(2) My editor at McGraw-Hill has been fired. The situation in the trade book department there is total confusion.

(3) Tib Sherrill still can't (won't) be my editor. She's taken on other assignments: she thinks the *Gloria* project is wrong for me.

(4) The writing of *Gloria* is not developing as it should.

(5) Len's commuting to New York every other week puts an extra burden on me to be both mother and part-time father to Jeff and Chester (though I have to remind myself that our living in Florida is Len's accommodation to my fragile health).

(6) Linda's graduation from Ohio Wesleyan was not a happy occasion. The Vietnam War has many young people in our nation in a state of rebellion, including Linda.

(7) My relationships with Peter and Edith are not good. They resist almost every suggestion I make.

(8) Since U.S. troops have gone into Cambodia our college and university campuses are rioting, buildings being burned. We in the U.S. are a fragmented people, unable to hear one another.

O Jesus, You who cursed the fig tree so that, being un-productive, it withered and died, You who create, but must, at times, also destroy, I thank You that what is of God in all this will emerge.

Section II
The Summer
of 1971

Editor's Note: Catherine did little writing in her journals during this time. This section is based on twenty hours of tapes recorded by Catherine and me in September 1971, plus recollections by some of those involved in the events.

A Call to Do Battle _____

*E*dith ... Amy Catherine Marshall entered the world in the middle of the afternoon on July 22, 1971. Peter and I had again traveled to the Goddard Hospital in Stoughton, seventy miles from home, so that we could have the kind of childbirth experience we wanted. We were thrilled to be having another baby, never imagining that there might be a problem again.

This time Peter was permitted into the delivery room. My labor was normal from every point of view. But as soon as Amy was born I knew that something was wrong. The doctor didn't hold her up for us to see. He didn't put her on my breast while he cut the cord. She didn't cry. There was a scurrying among the nurses and a muffled hush that didn't ring true to my experience with Mary Elizabeth's birth. From my stirruped position on the table, I looked to the left where she was being bundled.

"Is she OK?" I asked.

"Well, she's a little blue. We're going to put her under a heat lamp and warm her up. I'm sure she'll be fine." But the doctor was grim-faced and nobody seemed to be looking at me. Peter kept patting my arm. They whisked her away to the nursery, saying she should have a little oxygen.

Throughout the evening, the nurses kept making excuses for not bringing Amy to me. She was having a little bit of trouble, they'd say.

"What's the matter?" I'd want to know.

"The pediatrician is looking her over now. He'll be in to talk with you a little later."

With every little bit of information I could glean, the reality was ever-so-slowly breaking through. My baby was not all right. She had poor muscle tone. She wasn't sucking. She wasn't wetting. She had a yellowish cast they needed to monitor. She was being fed fluids intravenously.

No, no, no. Every brain cell resisted taking it in. It couldn't be happening again. It couldn't be true. But it *was* true. And finally tears held back by a dam of denial came spilling out, uncontrollably, along with anguished questioning—why, why, why?

An angel of mercy visited me late on the first night. She was a nurse going off duty who had recognized our name on the patient sheet and knew that I would welcome prayer. She crept into my darkened room and sat next to the bed, taking my hand in hers. What she prayed I don't remember, but it provided for me the unmistakable assurance that God had not forgotten and that I could count on His presence even in my darkest, angriest, most despairing hour.

The next morning the pediatrician came again. He said

he'd noticed on my chart that we had previously lost an infant son. Would I authorize a release of those autopsy reports? They might have some bearing on a diagnostic assessment for Amy. He also felt the baby should be transferred to Boston Children's Hospital. They had good diagnostic capabilities there; would I authorize transferral and transportation in an ambulance?

Within a couple of hours a brisk young resident from Children's Hospital, Dr. Rubinstein, came to take Amy away. I watched from my second-story window as the tiny bassinet was loaded into the cavernous expanse of the shiny ambulance. The little body that I had never nestled in my arms was surrounded by hanging bottles and monitoring equipment. Technology was taking my place. Such feelings of uselessness were to recur often in the weeks ahead. With lights flashing the ambulance raced away.

The first hint that the doctors suspected a genetically related disease came the next day. Dr. Rubinstein came to see me armed with all kinds of questions about infant deaths in the family tree. He explained that they were seeing exactly the same symptomatology in Amy Catherine that existed with Peter Christopher four-and-a-half years before.

Now through a computerized search the doctors at Children's believed they had a diagnosis: an extremely rare, recessively inherited, genetically carried disease. This disease, Dr. Rubinstein explained, is manifested in babies as a result of defective genes, which both mother and father have to contribute in order to result in—I heard for the first time the dreaded name—cerebro-hepato-renal syndrome. Apparently the defective genes control the pathway of migrating cells during embryonic development. Should two defective genes meet at conception (a one-in-four probability in affected persons), proper migration of embryonic cells to the brain, liver, and kidneys is impeded and as a result these organs are malformed and virtually nonfunctional in the full-term infant.

Dr. Rubinstein concluded his explanation by saying that there had been only forty recorded cases of this disease, and that none of those forty infants had survived. Indeed, survival much beyond six months was impossible, given the fact that the brain was so incapacitated that it could not support life. His best guess was that Amy might live five to ten weeks.

There it was: cold, clinical reality. Overwhelmed, I longed to go home, to the stable life I knew of cooking for Peter and playing dolls with Mary, of raising vegetables and cutting flowers, of Sunday school teaching and singing in the choir. To life when "cerebro-hepato-renal syndrome" was just a string of unpronounceable syllables.

Catherine ... Edith came home without the baby just as Len and I arrived from Florida by automobile. We explained to two-and-a-half-year-old Mary Elizabeth that Amy Catherine was sick and had to stay in the hospital.

Then we began to phone praying friends around the country. Peter used some previously scheduled speaking engagements to talk about Amy Catherine's condition and ask for prayer. On Sunday, four days after she was born, Peter asked his congregation in East Dennis to pray for the healing of his baby daughter.

The Marshalls had a sixteen-year-old girl named Debbie living with them to look after Mary Elizabeth and help around the house. The discussion about the table on Sunday evening focused on how negative all the medical personnel at Children's Hospital were about Amy Catherine's chances.

The weight of our negativism and anguish must have gotten to Debbie. In the middle of the night she became so sick to her stomach that at 4:30 A.M. Len drove her to the Hyannis Hospital. There she was medicated and released, with instructions to rest for several days.

Monday was unbelievable. First the dishwasher broke down, then the hot water heater. For two days we were without hot water. Edith, only five days after childbirth, had to minister to Debbie, answer a steady stream of telephone calls, and supervise the household, while I took care of Mary Elizabeth.

To top it off, Peter's car wouldn't start and he had to spend most of the day getting it repaired.

By Tuesday morning at breakfast time we were all so beaten by this string of mishaps that a spontaneous prayer rose from the table: "Lord, we need help."

The answer came in a totally unexpected way. Some ten miles further down the Cape, in Orleans, the leaders of a Christian community responded to the need of the Marshalls. Two women were dispatched in a van with enough food for two meals. They told us later that they had started out from Rock Harbor singing and praising God. The closer they got to East Dennis and to the Marshall home the darker the atmosphere got and the harder they found it to sing and pray. "It was as if we were coming against some kind of strange powerful force."

They arrived cheerily enough, bringing the food in from the van. Then they cleaned the house from top to bottom, cooked and washed dishes and took charge of the telephone, leaving Peter, Edith, Len, and me free to have long sessions of prayer that afternoon and evening.

The first prayer session was in Peter and Edith's bedroom, chosen not only because Edith could participate while lying down, but also because it was the only room with air-conditioning. We began by praying for that tiny, precious life at Boston Hospital.

Then I described how I'd been awakened in the middle of the night by the Lord who revealed to me why all my life I'd seen so few results of my prayers for healing—either my own or others'. "I was told that it was because I have a great fear of disease," I said, "and that if I could get rid of this fear then I could be better used by the Lord in praying for Amy Catherine."

"Perhaps," Edith suggested, "we can inherit fears as well as illness." She and Peter had been given some long forms to fill out by the geneticist at Children's Hospital. On these forms they were supposed to record not only the physical disabilities of their ancestors on both sides of the family, but the phobias, too—since apparently even these things can come down from generation to generation.

This led us to Exodus 20:5: ". . . For I, the Lord your God, am a jealous God, visiting the iniquity of the fathers on the children, on the third and the fourth generations" (NIV).

"Then," I said, "if I'm to get rid of my fear of disease I may have to look back to my parents and grandparents."

Immediately I found myself recalling my father's mother, Sarah Wood, for whom I'd been named. Sarah Catherine Wood was a name I'd disliked and seldom used.

Why had I resisted using the name *Sarah*?

As it dawned on me, I felt chills racing up and down my back. My Grandmother Wood had been so afraid of the night air that she wouldn't raise her bedroom window, winter or summer. In hot weather my grandfather would come out of their room in the morning white-faced and dripping with perspiration. After he died, my grandmother persuaded my Aunt Effie to sleep with her—with the same results.

Grandmother Wood was so afraid of thunderstorms that at the first peal she would plunge beneath the covers. And so it went. A fear-dominated woman.

In going back through my own life, I came up with a time when my specific fear of germs began. It was when we lived in West Virginia. Next door to us was a family named Fletcher whose Victorian home had a number of porches upstairs and down. The Fletcher boy was dying of tuberculosis. He used to lie out on the top porch where from my bedroom I could hear his terrible hacking cough. Then his sister caught the disease, ending up in the Trudeau sanatorium in New York State. This close association with lingering death planted in me a morbid fear of "contamination."

There in the bedroom Len and Peter laid hands on me and prayed that I be cut loose, in the spirit, from both inherited fears and acquired ones.

Next Peter began probing for the roots of his own fears. He recalled that around the time of his father's death, when he was nine, he had been harassed by some older boys on our block. Since he couldn't stand up to these bigger boys, he would end up running home. This memory still haunted him.

Peter's favorite Old Testament hero, he told us, was the young boy David, going out to fight the giant Goliath. "I would love to have this quality in me, this fearlessness," he said. "The ability to stand up against superior odds and not run away."

I found myself almost catapulted across the room toward my son. Laying my hands on Peter's head, I prayed this prayer: "My son, I hereby cut you free from me, from any fears of mine that would bind you in any way. Even as Samuel anointed David, so I now anoint you to go out and fulfill your appointed destiny in life boldly, whatever that may be."

Peter told me afterward that he felt something very real happened to him during this prayer, something he had been needing for a long time.

Our second family session took place in the living room after dinner. We invited Pat, a neighbor of the Marshalls, to join us because of her experience as an intercessor. We had also invited her for dinner, but she had declined. "I'm on a fast for Amy Catherine," she told us.

After we had prayed together, Pat had a strong message for us. First, we had to overcome the discouragement brought on by the medical diagnosis. Second, we had to fight for Amy Catherine's life. "The word I've received from the Lord is that Amy Catherine is a member of the Body of

Christ—a member in need of ministry. You have no right to deprive her of this ministry or back away from it, no matter what the doctors say."

These words hit me like a slap in the face. A call to battle! All my adrenaline began to flow.

Peter and I drove to Boston the next day, Wednesday. At last I was to have my first visit with Amy Catherine, now one week old. She was in a special section of Children's Hospital for babies with rare diseases. As we entered the medical complex through double swinging doors, we passed a large bulletin board covered with snapshots of babies and small children. A printed sign above it read *Our Graduates.*

This gave us a good feeling, indicating that there was a personal touch in this hospital, that it was not just a sterile treatment center. We had to put on gowns, though not masks, and scrub our hands with a particular kind of soap. Meanwhile the nurse in charge had picked up the baby, wrapping her in a tiny blanket, and was waiting to place her in our arms.

"We've come to pray for Amy Catherine's healing," I told her.

The nurse had been smiling. Now her expression changed. "The doctor has explained to you the prognosis, hasn't he?"

We nodded.

"The baby has many problems. There have been multiple seizures. Please don't get your hopes up."

"We believe God will heal her," Peter said firmly.

Peter carried Amy Catherine into a glassed-in small room where he anointed his tiny daughter with the oil he had brought with him. Then he placed her in my arms. I unfolded a corner of the blanket. She was such a beautiful baby, with her rosebud mouth, delicately shaped head, rose-petal skin. She did not open her eyes as my tears fell on her blanket.

Peter . . . The first crisis with Amy Catherine had come 36 hours after her birth when she still had not wet her diapers. This meant no kidney function, without which she would not live another day.

We'd called every prayer group we could think of to intercede for her. Members of my own church went into a special session. One prayer warrior there had a vision of an arterial system with vessels branching out from it like limbs of a tree. Then she saw fluid begin to work through the system. It was soon after this that Amy Catherine's kidneys had begun to function.

We had rejoiced. God had responded!

The Gathering
of Sixteen _____

Catherine ... On August 1, 1971, the second Sunday after Amy Catherine's birth, my son after much prayer mounted the pulpit of his East Dennis church and preached a sermon that rocked all of us. The subject was faith and the substance of it was this:

As you all know, my daughter Amy Catherine was born on July 22nd with severe genetic problems in her liver, kidneys, and brain. The doctors have given us no hope that she will live more than a few weeks. In fact, no baby with this genetic syndrome has ever lived beyond six months.

I am here to state this morning that the doctors do not have all the answers. Our Lord God does. He is the Creator of life. He decides when we are born and when we die.

I do not know what His plan is for Amy Catherine. But I do know that we are to believe for her healing. In fact, right here now before you all, and God almighty, I claim a miracle of healing for Amy Catherine.

I was sitting next to Edith during the service and felt her pride in him at that moment. Later I discovered that others in the congregation were troubled by the sermon because he'd left no loophole in case the baby died. But to me there was something very moving in the way my son stuck his chin out and said, "Lord, I believe."

Peter's sermon, plus Pat's exhortation to us, sparked something inside me. We had received our marching orders. *The time had come for action!*

What if our family crisis with Amy Catherine was part of the movement of the Holy Spirit sweeping across the country in 1971? Len and Jeffrey had recently returned from California to report the Jesus Movement among young people gaining momentum. *Guideposts* was putting together a special series of articles to be called "The Surging Spirit."

What if a miraculous healing of this "hopeless" situation was part of the Spirit's mighty plan for the '70s? Then the idea came: *Call together some prayer warriors. Have them come to Cape Cod to pray for Amy Catherine, to claim a supernatural healing!*

Len and I got on the telephone. Those we called were asked to come the following Sunday for a four-day, all-out prayer campaign. The place—yet to be decided. Probably somewhere on the Cape; possibly nearer Boston so we would be closer to Children's Hospital.

Edith . . . I seized eagerly on Mom's and Len's offer to gather some prayer warriors together to battle Amy's sickness. The fact that they were taking the initiative was especially welcome, for I was feeling helpless and inadequate.

Life seemed to have reeled out of control. It had nightmarish qualities about it. I couldn't do any of the things that to me seemed important, like nursing my newborn infant and helping Mary Elizabeth through this crisis and regaining my own strength and standing together with Peter to make decisions. Amy was hooked up to machines in a hospital ninety miles away, I was exhausted from the constant trips into Boston, and I couldn't seem to get a very good handle on all the "input" that loving and well-meaning Christian brothers and sisters were giving us. In addition to everything else, I was beginning to wonder if maybe there was something dreadfully wrong with me spiritually.

And so, if others would take up the slack in the battle lines and let me regain some equilibrium, I was only too glad to have them do it.

Catherine . . . Soon the details of the gathering on Cape Cod were worked out, both as to place and people. A Christian center in Orleans soon to be named the Community of Jesus offered its facilities: Rock Harbor Manor, a lovely location on Cape Cod Bay with sleeping accommodations and spacious meeting rooms. The two women who came to the Marshall home the previous Tuesday to clean, cook, and minister were from this community.

The people who responded to our calls made an unusual mix: John and Elizabeth Sherrill were long-time friends; Jamie Buckingham, a roving editor for *Guideposts*, was a new friend. Virginia Lively was a prayer partner of mine in Florida and a woman with a nationwide ministry of healing. Charles Hotchkiss, who came with his wife, Linda, was Virginia's pastor and an Episcopal priest in Belle Glade.

Bob Slosser was a *New York Times* editor; with him came his wife, Gloria. Scott and Nedra Ross had a Christian ministry to young people in upstate New York. These last two couples were close friends of the Sherrills. We invited Arthur Gordon, a close *Guideposts* associate, and his wife, Pam. Arthur couldn't come, but Pam did.

The final person invited was our 22-year-old daughter Linda. She was working in her Grandmother LeSourd's gift shop in Maine when I called her. Linda and I had gone through some difficult times in our twelve-year step-mother/stepdaughter relationship, but the Lord impressed her name unmistakably on my mind. Linda later told me she probably would not have come unless I personally had asked her.

By Sunday afternoon, August 8, all of these people had gathered at Rock Harbor Manor. Counting Peter and Edith, we totaled sixteen. It soon became clear, however, that there was anything but close compatibility among us. "Lord," I found myself praying, "are You sure these are the people You summoned here?"

Virginia Lively . . . The call from Catherine came in early August: her newborn granddaughter lay in critical condition at Children's Hospital in Boston. However, Catherine went on, God had told her that if a group of prayer warriors gathered on Cape Cod and prayed for a miracle, the Lord would heal this child. Would I be willing to come?

How could I refuse? I loved Catherine, and my heart ached for her family. I assured Catherine that I would come to the Cape.

As soon as I got off the phone, I knelt by my bed to pray. I believed implicitly in Jesus' desire to heal Amy Catherine; and Catherine had told me on the phone that God had promised to do this if we would ask in faith. But now, even before I began to pray for Amy Catherine and for Peter and Edith, I heard the inner voice I had come to know so well:

This child will not live. But any other child they have they may have in perfect confidence.

I was stunned. Never in twenty years of healing ministry had I received such a totally unexpected message from God—a message of great promise linked with a message of death. Why? I was investing my entire life in the belief that Jesus wanted to heal. Why would He choose not to restore a tiny newborn?

As I continued to kneel beside my bed, my mind reeled with questions. Could this message really be from God? It stood in direct opposition to the divine assurance Catherine believed she had received. Had I mistaken something else for the voice I thought I knew? If not—if I had actually heard from God—should I relay the message to Catherine, challenging her own spiritual discernment? In any case, was this the proper time to reveal so hard a word from God, as she was undergoing a wrenching family crisis? Shouldn't I simply wait and let events prove or disprove the message? God could reveal His will to Catherine in His own way, in His own time, without any help from me.

"Lord, is this message from You?" I asked.

Flooding me came the assurance that it was. "Then what do You want me to do with it? Do You want me to share it with Catherine? With the others at Cape Cod? I need Your wisdom, Lord."

For as long as I knelt by my bed, I heard nothing more.

I had come to the Lord back in 1951, with neither questions nor expectations, giving myself completely, wherever that might lead. He in turn had used me as a channel to bring His healing to others. Despite my previous suspicion of Christians who tossed off references to "hearing the Lord" as glibly as I might refer to a conversation with a neighbor, in the years that followed I had learned to distinguish His thoughts from my own. The inner voice, though inaudible, was very clear. There was His admonition, for example, to grieve for three days after my husband Ed passed away, then to let him go to his new life and I to mine.

There was one message I had *not* heard, however, which was coming to represent the biggest trial of my Christian life: I also had a daughter named Linda. For years I had been praying for her healing from an illness with symptoms of dizziness and lack of energy that seemed to defy diagnosis. With no results.

I knew by heart the Bible promises of healing, like verses 2–3 from Psalm 103:

> Bless the Lord, O my soul,
>   and forget not all his benefits,
> who forgiveth all thine iniquities,
>   who healeth *all thy diseases*. . . .
>   KJV

God said right in His Word that He would heal *all* our diseases. So why didn't He heal my Linda? I certainly believed He could heal her, just as He healed many through my own hands. But after thirteen years, Linda seemed no closer to healing than she had in the pediatrician's office as a pre-teen. My daughter continued to suffer this nameless affliction while I carried on a healing ministry! "I've seen You do so many miracles, Lord," I prayed with growing urgency. "When will You do this one?"

The Clarion Call _____

*L*en ... From the very first Monday morning meeting of
the sixteen in the spacious lounge of Rock Harbor Manor,
there was divergence among us. When some of the group
admitted that they had come for the fellowship as well as
for the immediate emergency, Catherine reacted sharply.

"The purpose of this get-together," she declared, eyes
flashing, "is to pray for a miracle. The word from the Lord is
that if we would gather a group here to pray for Amy
Catherine, the power of His Spirit will fall on us and Amy
Catherine will be healed."

I stared at Catherine in amazement. During our prayers
together for the baby she had never sounded so confident.
Her all-out faith picked up where her son's sermon the

week before had left off. I looked at the circle of faces
focused on Catherine. Their expressions ranged from Peter's nodding approval to Virginia Lively's look of strange
anguish to Gloria Slosser's stark amazement to a "let's-go-
for-it" exuberance on the face of Charles Hotchkiss.

What a strange mixture of people, I thought to myself.
Already it was clear that pastors Hotchkiss and Marshall
would be strong, aggressive leaders; both had experience in
healing ministries. But Catherine's clarion call for boldness
of faith surprised me because of her long frustration in this
area. "I certainly do not have the gift of healing," she often
lamented, after vainly storming heaven for an ailing friend
or relative. I surmised that what had changed her was that
prayer time in the Marshalls' bedroom when she identified
the roots of an abnormal fear of disease, and Peter and I
claimed freedom for her.

A tremor of excitement shot through me. If God had
promised Catherine a supernatural healing of Amy Catherine, this was going to be a momentous occasion.

My eyes moved about the room. The look on Linda's face
was inscrutable. I didn't know my daughter very well. I was
glad she was here.

John and Elizabeth Sherrill remained intimate friends,
inextricably involved in Catherine's and my lives. Since
Tib's negative reaction to the *Gloria* project, the relationship had suffered. Yet in this crisis Catherine had turned
instinctively to them.

The Slossers and Rosses were friends of the Sherrills. "I
think they will make a contribution," was John's simple
explanation for inviting them. As a *New York Times* reporter, Bob Slosser seemed a most unlikely prayer warrior,
yet we were to find his practical wisdom and sensitive
spirit a good balance during the emotional scenes that were
to occur. His wife, Gloria, was one of those quiet intercessors from whom power radiates.

Scott Ross, son of a Scottish Presbyterian preacher, in-

trigued me. In reaction against what he saw as the hypoc-
risy of the Church, Scott had turned to a "hippie" lifestyle,
becoming a popular disc jockey, an intimate of the Beatles
and the Rolling Stones. After his conversion he and his
wife, Nedra, had started a ministry called Love-Inn: a large
farmhouse in upstate New York where rebellious young
people could "live in" for a period and encounter Jesus
Christ.

How fascinating that Bob Slosser and Scott Ross some
seventeen years later would have leading roles at the Christian Broadcasting Network, Bob as President of CBN University and Scott as a 700 Club interviewer.

Jamie Buckingham, formerly a Baptist minister, had become a roving editor for Guideposts after the Sherrills discovered his outstanding writing talent at the 1967
Guideposts Writers Workshop.

Linda Hotchkiss, like Gloria Slosser, was the kind of
strong intercessor whose work would undergird all that
was to come. Pam Gordon would be arriving that afternoon
by plane. As perhaps the newest believer among us, she was
to perform a mission she would never have contemplated.

As I studied these people and their various gifts, my own
role seemed obvious. Someone was needed to handle the
myriad details behind the scenes. As the executive editor
of Guideposts, seeing that other people got their jobs done
was a big part of my role. Working out the details of housing
and travel for this gathering had taken a lot of doing, and I
mentioned in that first session that it had required all my
skill as an organizer. To my dismay, instead of praise, this
simple statement drew fire.

"I think your focus here is wrong, Len," said John.

"What I'm picking up here is a managerial spirit," Jamie
concurred.

I was chagrined. "I wasn't complaining, just stating
facts," I said.

"Maybe," John persisted, "your concern for details is blocking the Holy Spirit from using you more in a ministry role."

"Len," Virginia Lively joined in, "I notice you're constantly looking at your watch. Your mind is not here. Is it on the plane you're supposed to meet—or perhaps the article you're writing for *Guideposts?*"

Edith Marshall spoke up. "I'll go meet Pam Gordon at the Hyannis Airport this afternoon. Len, you stay here and be a part of this body."

Later, as we prayed, the word came that three men should drive to Boston that afternoon to anoint Amy Catherine with oil. As an elder in the church, I should be one of the three.

Prayer for the baby followed. It began quietly, then grew in volume. "Thank You, Lord, for healing Amy Catherine. . . . We praise You, Lord, that You are doing a mighty work in her small body. . . . Hallelujah—right now the baby is being healed!"

The note was one of rejoicing. Why did it make me feel uneasy?

When Peter Marshall, Jamie Buckingham, and I arrived at Children's Hospital that afternoon, I found myself surprisingly nervous. I had never before anointed a person with oil for healing. In our Delray Beach Presbyterian church this was considered the pastor's role. Elders were expected to oversee finances and perform other mundane services. And yet the Scripture passage in James was perfectly clear:

> Is any sick among you? let him call for the elders of the church; and let them pray over him, anointing him with oil in the name of the Lord.
>
> James 5:14, KJV

Before going up to the children's ward, Peter, Jamie, and I stopped in at the chapel to pray. In the quiet beauty of that place I sensed that Jesus was looking on our efforts with love and compassion. He had certainly loved children during His time on earth. I had a surge of hope that we could be His instruments for healing Amy Catherine.

In the children's ward a nurse placed the tiny baby in my arms. I braced her awkwardly against one shoulder while I fumbled with the bottle of oil. As I moistened my fingers with several drops of oil, I wondered again why the least trained of the three of us should be doing this.

"Lord," I plunged in, "as an elder in the church and this baby's grandfather, I claim the promise of Your Word for Amy Catherine . . . I now anoint this small child of Yours and pray that a healing will take place in her body . . . in the name of Jesus."

It was a jittery performance by this grandfather. Sweat built up on my forehead and I nearly dropped the bottle of oil on the floor. My prayer was a stumbling sequence of uncertain words, so quietly uttered that a nurse and an orderly working on the other side of the room never even looked in our direction.

What I learned from that experience, though, has stayed with me ever since. *My willingness to perform a priestly function in my role as an elder in the church or head of my home is much more important than the skill with which I carry it out.*

Peter and Jamie held Amy Catherine in turn, cradling her tenderly in their arms and praying for her. Human beings invoking God for a miracle. *Lord,* I wondered, *just how important is our role in what You will do here?*

Then the thought struck me. I remembered the prayers of the group that morning, releasing me from a managerial spirit to assume a fuller role in the Body of Christ. Perhaps our ministry to Amy Catherine was not the only thing God wanted from us in the next few days.

Jamie . . . The afternoon we went into the hospital to pray for Amy Catherine I slipped away from Len and Peter to make another prayer visit. A couple of years before I had met a New England couple, Jim and Linda Byrd, who were thinking of moving to Florida. We had corresponded several times. In her last letter Linda had asked me to pray for the child of a dear friend. The little girl was dying of cystic fibrosis and had been taken to Children's Hospital in Boston.

I had prayed, but had forgotten the whereabouts of the child until the afternoon we drove from Cape Cod to Boston to pray for Amy Catherine. Suddenly it occurred to me that this other child—a little girl of eight or nine—was in this very hospital.

After our prayer time with the Marshall infant I excused myself and checked at the nurses' station. Yes, the little girl I was concerned about was located just down the hall.

I found the room and knocked gently. There was no answer, but I could hear activity beyond the door. I eased the door open and realized why no one had heard me. An emergency was taking place. The beautiful little red-haired child was lying on the bed, wired and tubed to all kinds of machines. Two nurses were working feverishly over her. Her mother was standing at the foot of the bed, weeping.

"I'm Jamie Buckingham," I whispered to her. "I'm from Florida and Linda—"

"Oh," she gasped. "You're a pastor, aren't you?"

I nodded. "What's happening here?" I asked.

"She stopped breathing. They've got her started now, but it could happen again at any time."

"Would you mind if I prayed for her?"

The young mother clung to my hand, her body still shuddering with sobs. I reached out with my other hand and laid it on the little girl's foot, protruding from under the sheet that had been pulled loose as the nurses thrashed about, bringing her back to life.

Suddenly the frantic activity stopped. The two nurses and the hospital attendant straightened up, looking at me for the first time, then bowed their heads. Even the machines in the room, gasping and gurgling, sucking and beeping, seemed to pause.

"Lord, heal this child in Jesus' name," I prayed.

It was brief. Just a few sentences, then I withdrew my hand and was gone.

It was not until after I returned to my home in Melbourne, Florida, more than a week later, that I got the news. Linda Byrd, who knew nothing of my visit, had called my wife. A miracle had happened, she reported. Remember the little girl with cystic fibrosis who had been dying in the Boston hospital? Well, she had just been released, allowed to go home. The doctors said they must have made a mistake. It wasn't cystic fibrosis after all—because that's incurable. And the child was fine now. Healed completely. She thought we'd want to know.

The Slugger _____

Catherine . . . The moment Scott and Nedra Ross arrived, a struggle began inside me. I was aware of an inability to relate to them, which troubled me. Unless we were united as a praying body, would the Lord honor our prayers for Amy Catherine's healing?

Scott, I learned, had been born in Scotland to an evangelical preacher's family. That part intrigued me, for I had loved the Scottish people ever since my marriage to Peter Marshall. But when his family emigrated to America, Scott found himself—kilts, accent, kitchen table haircut—the butt of cruel teasing on the school playground. Worse, the small church his father had come to pastor broke every promise they had made to his simple, unworldly parents.

Before long Scott had shed his Scottish accent and his church background eventually to become a disc jockey with a focus on rock music.

Nedra, a beauty with both black and Indian blood, had a gift of spiritual discernment, which would emerge during the days that followed. The Sherrills were so high on the Rosses that they were doing a book with Scott that would soon be published under the title *Scott Free*.

Why was I resistant to them? The generation gap again . . . and yet the Sherrills are in the same generation Len and I are. Was it because I saw how our Linda was drawn to them? Because I sensed the attraction of rebellious spirits to each other?

The meeting on Tuesday morning took place outdoors on the lawn adjacent to Rock Harbor Manor. It began with a report on the trip to Boston by the three men. The nurses had been most cooperative as the three ministered to the baby; the condition of Amy Catherine was unchanged. Peter reaffirmed his belief that the Lord was going to perform a miraculous healing in his daughter.

After this positive opening, the tenor of the meeting changed. Peter offered to the group a Scripture passage he felt had been given him:

> And he shall enter into a strong and firm covenant with the many for one week; and in the midst of the week he shall cause the sacrifice and offering to cease; and upon the wing or pinnacle of abominations [shall come] one who makes desolate; until the full determined end is poured out on the desolator.
>
> Daniel 9:27, AMPLIFIED

This seemed to us a very strange passage of Scripture to apply to the present situation. It was to haunt some of us in the weeks that followed.

Peter then bluntly asked a question: Were we all supposed to be here? There was an uncomfortable silence; then somewhat defensively people began to share. One of the first to do so was Scott Ross.

Scott vividly described what it was like to be a preacher's kid in a strange land . . . the loneliness, the poverty, the rejection. Bitterly he lashed out against the Church, which had mistreated them. "The leadership of the established Church is phony. They don't care about the people, they don't care about the clergy. They don't care that the pastor of a small church and his family hardly have enough to eat. They serve themselves and their own pet projects. They're a group of hypocrites. . . ." His voice rose despairingly. "The church is nothing but vomit. It's . . . it's dog's vomit."

It was too much. I found myself on my feet, pointing a finger at Scott. "How dare you call the Body of Christ 'dog's vomit'! How dare you say that about the Church that Jesus said was His Body and for which He died! How can you say such a thing and still call yourself a Christian?"

My outburst was totally spontaneous. I was propelled to my feet without any conscious decision. What happened then was completely unexpected.

Instead of lashing back at me and defending his statements, a dam seemed to break inside of Scott. Tears streaming from his eyes, he began to sob convulsively. The cleansing lasted a long, long time. With Virginia Lively laying hands on his head, and me holding his hand, Scott was freed from the spirit of hatred that had taken root in him as a small, bewildered boy.

A healing also took place inside me as my habitual negativism about the lifestyle he represented dissolved, for once, in understanding.

Another surprising event took place during that same morning meeting. We'd agreed that each afternoon a contingent representing the group would drive to Boston to pray on the spot for Amy Catherine during the hospital visiting hours. The question arose: Whom should it be today?

We had a quiet time of prayer, then Jamie Buckingham broke the silence. "I feel that God has given me the name of one person He wants to go to Children's Hospital today— Pam Gordon."

I will never forget the kaleidoscope reaction on Pam's face: first incredulity, then fear, then pain. Finally, a torrent of tears. As with Scott Ross, some of us gathered about Pam to minister to her as she kept repeating, "I'm not worthy . . . I'm just not worthy . . . ."

"Being worthy has nothing to do with it," Jamie tried to explain.

Being asked to go and pray for a newborn baby girl, to hold her in her arms, had clearly opened up an old traumatic wound in Pam's heart. The tears and prayers that followed were the beginning of a second healing on that sunlit patch of lawn that morning.

The explosion of emotions had been so physically tiring, however, that I went to my room right after lunch to take a nap, leaving it to the group to decide who would accompany Pam Gordon to Boston.

Len . . . Most of us met again after lunch. We would have done better to have rested for an hour because there was little togetherness. Linda was upset about something. She and Scott Ross went off together to talk. The others couldn't agree on who should go to Boston and who should stay behind to support them in prayer. Pam, of course, was going. Edith said she had to go and finally Linda Hotchkiss became the third.

So ironic this selection, because we had spent much time that morning on the husband's role in spiritual leadership. Now here were three women on their way to Boston while the men went off to rest.

I went to our room where Catherine had gone right after lunch. "Who's going to Boston?" she asked sleepily.

"Pam, Edith, and Linda Hotchkiss."

Catherine jerked herself up to a sitting position. "You've got to be kidding!"

"That's the way it ended up. They're already on their way."

"What happened to the men?"

"None felt led."

"What about you—why didn't you object?"

"I was stripped of my managerial baton yesterday, remember?"

"And what about Virginia? She told me she felt she was supposed to go."

"The group chose Linda Hotchkiss."

To my surprise Catherine jumped out of bed and hurriedly began to dress.

"Where are you going?"

"I don't know. But three women going in to pray alone. Where's the spiritual authority there?"

"So you and Virginia will make five women."

"You're full of resentment, Len."

"No, I'm not. I had a great experience yesterday with Amy Catherine. It's changed my whole way of thinking about my role as a male. The men are copping out today because they're tired. You ducked out of the meeting after lunch because you were tired. So don't pass judgment."

She glared at me for a moment and stormed out of the room. I learned later what happened. Catherine went first to Virginia's room, got her up, then tracked down Peter and Charles Hotchkiss. Jamie joined them in the hall. Catherine lit into the men on the matter of their being "prophet, priest, and king" in intercessory situations. Soon Virginia, Peter, Charles, and Jamie were on their way to Boston, while

Catherine called the hospital and left word that the three women were to await the arrival of this second group.

The seven had a good prayer time at the hospital. They also agreed on a nickname for Catherine: "The Slugger."

Catherine . . . The next healing in the group occurred between John Sherrill and myself. Seven of us—Virginia Lively, Charles and Linda Hotchkiss, John and Tib Sherrill, and Len and me—had met in a special prayer session for Amy Catherine, little suspecting that a very different kind of restoration was going to take place.

After John Sherrill's experience of the Holy Spirit in Atlantic City back in 1962, a powerful ministry of teaching had begun for John. Often when he spoke of Jesus, he would choke up and have to struggle for composure, a sign of his close relationship with the Lord.

Four or five years after his baptism, I was dismayed to learn that John was going to a psychiatrist two or three sessions a week. When I challenged John on it, he stared at me in genuine bewilderment. John's entire family, he reminded me, had been active in the field of psychiatry for decades. His father, a seminary professor, had pioneered early efforts to reconcile religion and psychiatry. His mother and his sister (and Tib's sister, too) were psychiatric social workers. To John, psychiatry represented a medical breakthrough similar to—say—the discovery of the circulation of the blood. He couldn't see that going to a psychiatrist subtracted anything at all from his witness.

"But John," I protested, "you are switching authority figures in your life, substituting the psychiatrist for Jesus."

Again that baffled look. "Catherine, the doctor doesn't try to replace God! On the contrary—he can help someone find God, sort out neurotic ideas and holdovers from childhood, thus discover who Jesus really is."

"I've nothing against Christian psychiatrists," I agreed. "I know they can help people. But not you, John! My spirit rails against it for you."

As usual I came on too strong. A barrier went up between John and me, invisible, unacknowledged, but very real. On the surface the LeSourd-Sherrill relationship continued strong. Tib remained my editor—at least up to the *Gloria* project. We remained friends. Two years previously, in 1969, when Len and I returned to Kauai to celebrate our tenth anniversary in the same hotel where we'd spent our honeymoon, it was the Sherrills we invited to come with us. Still, I ached for the return of the old transparency among us.

Now, on Cape Cod, John prefaced our prayer time with this announcement: "You will be interested to know about a decision I've recently made, Catherine. I've concluded that I've made about all the progress I can in my psychiatric sessions. I'm grateful for the self-understanding I've gained, but I've decided that it's time to phase them out."

I was delighted to hear this, of course, but sensed that John had more to say.

John stroked his close-cropped beard for a long moment, then opened up. "You need to know that I've had a tremendous fear of making this break. The fear is not stopping the sessions *per se*, but of closing off the relationship. Twice before in my life when a major relationship was ruptured—by death in those earlier cases—the loss was followed by a bout with cancer. So now with this new separation I'm battling fear—the fear that the cancer will return."

Once he had gotten that fear out, John began to talk about the little boy John Sherrill, who had been skinny and not very athletic, growing up in a sports-centered Southern town. At this point, tears suddenly filled John's eyes.

Virginia Lively broke in. "The Lord has just given me these words for you: He says, 'John, I want you to know that *I will never* leave you; that you are and will always be one of My strong ones.'"

With this Virginia knelt before John and with great intensity of feeling said: "John, I wish I had the eloquent words to tell you the man that I see in you—the teacher, the leader, the prayer warrior, the communicator."

I sprang from my chair, moved across the room, and embraced him, saying: "John, I love you, I love you." By this time both John and I were weeping. There'd been a mystic, instantaneous reconciliation between him and me. I didn't quite understand what had happened or how; but my spirit was suddenly overflowing with joy in the reunion.

Something important was happening to the group through tears. Scott Ross had been embarrassed by his weeping, but healing inside him had begun the moment he let his emotions go. The same with Pam Gordon. And now John and me. The power and presence of God seemed to be in direct proportion to the tears that flowed. The men especially resisted this in our macho society where men are taught that it isn't "manly" to weep.

Yet we were discovering that tears were not to be feared, that often weeping opens the door to the *real* person inside and the reality of the situation to be dealt with. In fact, what we read in the Scripture about how God abhors hardness of heart should convince us that tears are the sign of the hard heart melting and therefore a very *true sign* of the Holy Spirit.

Still I went to bed that night troubled. Half of me was rejoicing over the restoration of my close relationship with the Sherrills, and over the other healings that were taking place. The other half of me was grieving over tiny Amy Catherine at the Boston hospital. Despite the massive prayer directed toward her, not only by our group of sixteen but from hundreds, perhaps thousands of people who had heard of her plight, there was no change in her condition.

What are we doing wrong, Lord? I asked silently, staring at the ceiling. *Are we missing something? Are we so busy talking to You and to each other that we're not listening for Your instructions to us?*

I turned toward Len to see if he was still awake. He was breathing steadily, asleep. How I envied his ability to drop off so quickly. The more I wanted to sleep, the harder it was for me to let myself go, as I endlessly replayed the day's events.

My dream that night turned out to be significant. It seemed there were two large houses that belonged to our family. There were many rooms in each house. Some were furnished, some were not. There was heirloom furniture in some of the rooms, but I was aware of the fact that a very great deal of work needed to be done in rearranging the furniture, adding new pieces, decorating. I was appalled at the task that lay before me and the rest of the family. Although other members of the family were about, the two main characters in the dream were my father and me.

Father's attitude in the dream was: we must get on with this refurbishing as quickly as possible. The episode seemed to be taking place rather late in Dad's life because he made the statement to me, "I'll stay with you to help as long as I possibly can." The fact that my father had passed away ten years before in 1961 didn't seem significant.

As I pondered this dream the next morning and then asked the Lord about it, I had the distinct impression that it referred to all the work that was going on in sorting out family relationships. Dad's repeated "Let's get on with it" stressed the urgency of this.

Linda _____

Catherine . . . The next morning, Wednesday, I opened the meeting with a plea that we stand together in spirit against the pessimistic opinions of the doctors and nurses at the hospital. There followed an hour's glorious prayer time for Amy Catherine. Powerful intercession. Strong affirmation that the baby was being healed.

Then came individual sharing. My stepdaughter, Linda, was sitting on the floor in front of her father. When I asked her where she was personally at this point, she singled out Scott and Nedra Ross as the two people who had been most helpful to her over the past few days.

"Do you need prayer, Linda?"

She shook her head a trifle uncertainly.

"How about a healing of any bad memories?" suggested Virginia Lively. "Maybe some that go back to when you were a small child?"

A long silence. "Well, there was a birthday when I was very little." She glanced up at her father.

Len had been writing something in his notebook. Now his head snapped up. "You remember your third birthday, Linda?" he asked.

"I'm not sure when it was. We were living in an apartment in Glen Oaks. You and Eve had a big fight—and you left."

Len was staring at her incredulously. "That was your third birthday."

"I guess so."

"Did you understand what the fight was all about?"

"No. I just remember that I had been so excited about having a birthday party. Then I was sent to my room to be all by myself, as though I were being punished. I couldn't understand this because I hadn't done anything wrong. I cried my heart out. Eve came in to comfort me after a while, but I felt you had deserted me, Dad."

As Len and Linda faced each other, suddenly my mind went back to the dream I had had the night before . . . the importance of restoring and redoing the rooms in our family house.

Len . . . I was stunned by Linda's revelation, amazed that she could remember that unpleasant scene after almost twenty years. I described to the group how her mother and I had decided to have a special cake, candles, ice cream, and presents for that third birthday party. I had arrived home at six P.M. to discover an empty vodka bottle and a wife who could hardly walk. I couldn't believe Eve would do that to her daughter. Not understanding the disease that alcoholism is, I blew up at her. The party was ruined. Linda was plunked back into her room and I was so frustrated that I stormed out of the house and just drove about aimlessly for the next two hours. Linda never did have her birthday party.

John Sherrill picked it up at that point. "Linda, what are your memories of your mother?"

"Mixed. I have some great memories of her. She taught me little songs and dances, took me places. We did a lot of things together. She was so beautiful, and I knew she loved me, but I didn't understand why she changed moods so quickly. There are some bad memories, too."

"Did her drinking upset you?"

"I wasn't always aware that she was drinking—just that she acted strangely at times."

I was getting increasingly uncomfortable over the way the meeting was going. "Are we getting off the track here with all these personal disclosures?" I asked.

John can be blunt. "I know this is unpleasant for you, Len, but I think we should hear Linda out on her bad memories." Then to my daughter, "Anything else you want to share?"

She was looking at me now. "Dad, I wasn't old enough to understand that Eve's drinking was the main problem. What I do remember is feeling so alone and hurt and torn up inside. Looking back, I can't help but wonder why no one ever seemed to care about what was going on inside of me.

"Dad, I love you so much . . . ." Her voice broke. After a pause she went on. "And I know you love me, but I feel like you've been gone a lot. Not just physically, but emotionally as well."

Catherine now spoke up. "Len, maybe there is something you need to look at here. Didn't you tell me once of a period in your life when you ducked out on any situation if it got emotional?"

I suddenly felt stricken. There *was* something here I needed to look at. "Yes, that's true. When I was around twelve I cried in a sad movie and was so embarrassed I remember giving myself an order that I would never cry again. For the next seventeen years I'd close off any encounter if I felt tears welling up."

"Is there still a tendency in you to duck out of tense situations rather than staying to see them through?" John asked.

"Perhaps."

"Can you think of any reason why emotion is hard for you to handle? How about your father? Was he like that?"

I shook my head. "My father was as close to being a saint as any man I ever knew." Then I checked myself. "Yes," I said. "There were times when my father retreated from unpleasant household scenes. My mother was inclined to get worked up at such times and burst into tears. I remember during these upsets of Mother's, Dad would go off and smoke a cigar. Only when Mother calmed down a little would Dad return and try to restore the peace."

"The generation thing again," said Catherine. "Do you see, Len, why we have called you 'the peacemaker' so often?"

"There's a difference between being a peacemaker and running away," said John.

"But inherited patterns can make someone like Len do both," suggested Catherine.

I knew what the conversation was leading to and was beginning to feel a deep inner agitation. My hands were trembling.

"Len, I guess what is coming out here concerns your divorce," said John gently. "Tib and I remember only too well the agony you went through with Eve, the years you spent trying to help her, the prayers we all poured into the situation. But, Len, maybe Linda isn't aware of all this. Maybe she thinks you just walked out on the marriage, like you walked out on her birthday party."

I leaned forward and touched Linda on the arm. "Is John right?"

Tears were sliding down her face. She nodded and leaned her head against my leg.

Words of protest formed in my mouth. Defensive, self-pitying words. Linda needed to know that the last five years of my marriage to her mother were the most painful experience of my life, that nothing, ever, could compare to the frustration, the anguish, the sheer bafflement of trying to help a loved one who was unable to accept help, who kept on the path of self destruction no matter what you did.

I stifled those words. Something deep in my spirit told me that Linda already knew of my pain, that she needed something else. My silent prayer: Lord, *what do I say to her?* Then the words came.

"Linda, the truth is that I did quit on the marriage. Will you forgive me?"

She nodded and reached for my hand. My tears joined hers as I hugged my daughter.

Linda ... I had come to Cape Cod not only because I was concerned for the baby, but also because Mom seemed to want me to come. Things had been very strained between us for as long as I could remember. The time with her at my college graduation had been awful. I felt we were worlds apart. Perhaps now Amy Catherine's need was providing a chance to find common ground. It was risky to be with Mom, for I wondered if she would ever accept me. And I was uneasy about being around Amy Catherine, as babies—sick or well—intimidated me. Yet my longing for family closeness propelled me to come—even over the protests of my Grandmother LeSourd, for whom I'd been working. In a strange way I even welcomed the fact that there was a crisis, for it seemed our family had experienced its greatest coming together in times of greatest pain.

After the emotional exchange between Dad and me on Wednesday morning I was about to take a shower. A particular moment is crystallized forever for me. I had one foot on the bathroom rug, the other in the bathtub. At that instant like a bolt of lightning the realization hit me that "one foot in, one foot out" was an accurate representation of my life. Several times in the past I'd gone through the motions of committing my life to the Lord, but always with part of me holding back.

Over the years I had sensed that God's hand was unmistakably in and on my life. But I resented the family pressure I felt toward Christianity. I was searching everywhere else for meaning in life, one time during college complaining in my journal, "Isn't there any choice for me but God?"

Standing half in, half out of the tub, suddenly I saw how He had allowed me to go my own way, had given me plenty of "rope," yet had always protected me from serious harm. Now it seemed He was saying to me, "Linda, it is time for you to decide—for Me, or against Me. You can no longer have it both ways."

At first I pulled back. Choosing the Lord's way would cost me, for some things in my life would have to change. And I doubted I would have much fun. But I couldn't bring myself to turn my back on Him entirely. Most of all, I was tired of living in two worlds and not enjoying either. I longed for peace and a sense of rightness about the direction of my life.

I took a deep breath and said aloud, "I choose You, Lord." Then I got into the shower. That shower was my point of no return.

Forbidden Feelings _____

*T*ib ... That summer of 1971 our own daughter, Liz, was fifteen. Eight years later, in God's strange ecology, Liz was to marry a geneticist, Alan Flint, who works in the research laboratory of Children's Hospital.

Until Children's new building was completed last year, anyone visiting Alan at his lab entered the hospital through the same Greek revival portico that once admitted us to Amy Catherine's ward. Each time I passed between those gray concrete pillars on Longwood Avenue the familiar feelings would sweep over me—sorrow, anger, pity, guilt. The emotions of 1971 still painfully alive in the 1980s.

They haunted me so long, I believe, because at the time these negative feelings were never expressed. I remember my vigils at Amy Catherine's cribside chiefly as times of grief denied. She was so tiny, so beautiful, so unequipped for this alien world. I remember holding her in a kind of awed astonishment, as though my human arms cradled a being from some unimaginably distant realm.

All babies bring with them a bit of eternity. But this one especially. Amy Catherine was wrapped in a stillness and inwardness that had nothing of this earth about it. I remember trying to pray, the first time John and I visited Amy, and being unable to form any image at all of this child joining our clamorous world.

John held the baby next and prayed for us both, affirming what we both knew to be true: God can reverse the direst medical prognosis.

And, yet, the tears I had not allowed to surface, there in the hospital, kept flowing in some hidden part of me throughout the four days on Cape Cod. Hidden but terribly real—the part of me that was heartsick and outraged, not only at this second ordeal for Edith and Peter, but at all the tiny sufferers occupying the cribs at Children's Hospital. The part of me that knew how Edith's heart was torn and twisted. The part that wanted to put my arms around her.

But gestures, even thoughts, of sympathy were ruled out by the premise of our gathering. I'd come fully assenting to that premise. "I tell you the truth," Jesus said, "if anyone says to this mountain, 'Go, throw yourself into the sea,' and does not doubt in his heart but believes that what he says will happen, it will be done for him."

In Amy Catherine's diagnosis we were indeed up against a mountain of impossibility. And we'd accepted the challenge, as a group and individually. We'd come to the Cape to claim the miracle promised to Catherine. But there was a condition to Jesus' promise: *We were not to doubt in our hearts.* Any admission of grief, even to myself, it seemed to me, was a form of doubt that could threaten the miracle's occurrence.

Agreeing together for the victory was the key. Absolute
unity was stressed so strongly that my unshed tears seemed
to me monstrous intruders in a sacred place. Again and
again I forced them down, berating myself for lack of faith.
Sometimes, across the room as we stormed heaven for the
baby's healing, I would see another tormented face and
imagine another struggle like my own.

But no one spoke out. No one questioned the victory
being proclaimed with such conviction. I hope it was not a
desire to get credit for a greater faith than I had that made
me keep silent. I don't think it was. I think it was a passion-
ate hope that those who sounded so sure of healing were
right. That my unexpressed sorrow was merely the result of
human-sized thinking.

And yet, as the days passed, a sense of unreality seemed
to steal over the impassioned prayers for Amy Catherine.
Years before, after Peter Christopher's death, Edith and I
had grown close during a stay at a retreat house in West
Germany. I'd loved the steel-sharp honesty that flashed
from her as she admitted, "I'm mad at God." Edith knew
that this was not a mature attitude. But she also knew that
gut-level reality is the road to maturity.

To all growth. It was happening again on Cape Cod. Out
of realness and honesty—however painful—was coming
healing for members of our group, time after time. Only in
our prayers for Amy Catherine were negatives ruled out.
Only in our prayers for her was power absent.

Edith . . . My overriding concern throughout the retreat was
my own spiritual state; if others were to be believed, there
was every indication that I must be dangerously "out of it."
After all, Peter had gone out on a limb, stating emphatically
and publicly that he believed God would heal Amy. And
Mom was crystal-clear that no other stance could possibly
line up with Scripture. Others in the group seemed to
concur. But in my heart of hearts, I wasn't sure I believed it.

Afraid that I was alone in my disbelief, I couldn't risk being honest. Adding to the confusion was the fact that part of me was genuinely afraid that any doubt on my part might keep God from being able to do His healing work.

So throughout the time, I worked hard at mustering up a mindset and a belief system that would not jeopardize our baby's well-being—as though by an act of my will I could change the message my own heart was receiving. Any doubt was 100 percent unacceptable, wasn't it? I could not, I must not, allow doubt any room or voice. My baby's life might be at stake.

The kinds of messages I was getting, which I believe were authentic, were ones having to do with Amy's need for love, for acceptance, for as many hours of cuddling as we could give her. Though the doctors had insisted that she had so little brain function she could not feel pain, I knew that in the midst of that jungle of wires, tubes, and monitors, her spirit was crying out for our unconditional love.

On the Beach _____

*C*atherine . . . By the third day it was obvious to all of us that the Holy Spirit had descended on our small group of sixteen. People had become painfully aware of their sins; tears of repentance were flowing, lives being redirected. To me, it was a prelude to the main event—the healing of Amy Catherine. "When, Lord?" I kept praying. "What is Your timing? Give us Your instructions."

Meanwhile, as the ministry continued in our group, several asked for a water baptism in the nearby bay. What some call a "believer's baptism"—baptism by total immersion after a personal step of commitment—had become popular during the current move of the Holy Spirit. Some of the men went down to the beach to scout out a suitable place for the ceremony.

Pam Gordon had returned from Children's Hospital glowing from her prayer time with Amy Catherine. "The baby smiled at me," she told us. "She really did." Pam was the first to ask for the "believer's baptism."

As we trooped down to the beach as a body, Pam confessed that all her life she had felt an overpowering fear of water. She had had a bad experience as a little girl when in fact she had almost drowned in a pond. Then as an older child there was another occasion when she nearly drowned. All of this had contributed to an almost paralyzing fear of allowing her head to go under the water.

To vacationers in swimming, or lounging on the sand, our proceedings must have presented a strange sight. Jamie was the first one immersed. Then came Peter. They had to find a deeper place in the water for Peter and it was quite something to see my son's tall form dipped beneath the surface. Next they baptized Edith. Then it was Pam's turn.

Jamie and Charles talked to her first, then prayed that the Lord would simply remove her fear. Which He did—gloriously. Pam was radiant as she came out of the water.

Jamie . . . When we walked down to the beach for water baptism that morning, I assumed that as a Baptist minister I would of course "officiate."

But God had other ideas and as the group left the house to make our way over the sand dunes and through the waist-high sea oats toward the water, I suddenly found myself in His presence. It was one of those rare times when I knew the Holy Spirit was teaching me. It developed into a dialogue as we headed toward the bay.

You're not going to do the baptizing, He said. The voice, although not audible, was just as real as if I had been standing in a classroom listening to a teacher.

"But I'm the most qualified. Besides, I want to. I *need* to." I had so little I could hold out as trophies to make others notice me.

*No, I am not going to let you do the baptizing, because
your own water baptism was out of order.*

I knew, of course, what He was talking about. It had
bothered me, on and off across the years, but like a lot of
other things that were not quite right, I had relegated it to
the back of my mind and tried to forget about it. During my
teenage years I had joined the First Baptist Church of Vero
Beach, Florida. In order to become a full member of the
church, I needed to be immersed—the outward sign, sup-
posedly, of an inward surrender to Christ. I talked to the
pastor and then on a Sunday morning, prodded by my
mother who also felt it was time for me to join a church, I
walked down the aisle and was received with what Bap-
tists call "the right hand of fellowship." A week later, on a
Sunday night, the pastor ushered me into the church bap-
tistry, suitably adorned in a white robe, and I was immersed.

But there had been no accompanying spiritual experience, no surrender of my will to Jesus Christ's. Even though
words to that effect were used, they were simply words. It
wasn't until several years later, when I found myself at a
campfire service on an island in Schroon Lake, New York,
that I made the necessary spiritual commitment to the
Lordship of Christ. Across the years ever since, I'd known
my water baptism had been premature.

But God is never finished with a man until he is con-
formed to the image of His Son. My baptism was one of
those things that I could no longer push beneath the surface
of my lake and pretend all was well. It was time to make the
correction. Publicly.

"But who will perform those baptisms if I don't?" I asked
the Holy Spirit.

Why, Charles Hotchkiss, who else? He responded.

I dreaded asking the next question for I already knew the
answer. "And who will baptize me?"

Charles Hotchkiss, the Spirit answered—and I could al-

most hear Him chuckle. *You'll be the first candidate when
we get to the bay.*

"But God!" I protested. "He's an Episcopal priest and I'm
a Southern Baptist minister."

This time it seemed the Holy Spirit laughed out loud.

However, in my obedience to the command of God, something else happened. In fact, it happened even before we
reached the water. I began to think of the sins I had
served—the substances that had controlled me. While
others might be addicted to alcohol or drugs, I was addicted to food. In short, I was a glutton. I was also fat. Not
"stocky," but blubbery fat. I carried around my waist more
than 25 pounds of excess flesh. I had been on every diet
imaginable, but all they did was set the stage for a subsequent weight gain.

I had resigned myself to remaining fat; yet deep inside I
knew I wasn't supposed to be that way. Now I began to
realize that water baptism was another key to inner healing,
for in submitting I was actually appropriating the death of
Christ to my own subconscious appetites:

> That like as Christ was raised up from the dead by the
> glory of the Father, even so we also should walk in newness
> of life.
>
> Romans 6:4, KJV

When we arrived at the water's edge, I pulled Father
Hotchkiss aside and made my rather unusual request. He
nodded, asked me a few questions, and agreed to take me
into the water first. He quickly made it plain that if I was to
submit to his baptizing me, I would also have to submit to
his method.

I had no sooner agreed than he turned to the group that
had assembled on the beach and said, "Jamie wants to go
first, but before I baptize him he wants to confess his sins
before you."

I hadn't counted on that. But I had come this far and meant to see it through. If my friends rejected me on the basis of my sins, that was their problem, not mine. I was determined to go all the way and leave my world under water.

So I named them: gluttony, lust, resentment, unforgiveness, pride, self-righteousness . . . on and on the list went. It was difficult and terribly embarrassing. If there was any group in the world I wanted to impress with my spirituality, this was it. Yet I knew God was pleased.

We waded out into the bay, which by that time was visibly receding. I crossed my hands in front of my chest, waiting for Father Hotchkiss to lower me backwards beneath the water.

"On your knees!" the priest said.

I started to protest, but I remembered that I had agreed to do it his way, no matter how strange it seemed. I dropped to my knees on the sandy bottom. The warm water came up to my chest. I felt the priest's hand on the back of my head and realized I was to go under face first.

I came up, shaking the water out of my ears, just in time to hear the priest say, "That's for the Father." Then, before I could catch a good breath, I was under again. This time the Son, and finally, a third time, for the Holy Spirit. I guess he figured he'd never get his hands on another Baptist minister.

Something did happen out there in the water, something in my inner spirit that had to do with discipline. I had begun a fast that day that I expected would last three days, which was the longest I had ever been without food. Instead, it lasted 28 days. During that time I began to experience a new surge of spiritual authority. Not only were my old appetites being broken, but by the time I returned home at the end of the week, I felt like Moses descending from Mt. Sinai with the tablets of stone in his hand and the radiance of God on his face. Apart from my experience with the baptism of the Holy Spirit, nothing had so visibly shaken and shaped my life as did my submission to baptism in the salty water of Cape Cod Bay.

Catherine . . . Thursday morning before sunrise the group met again on the beach, this time for a service of Communion. It was our final morning together, clear but cool; a covey of seagulls dove and swooped at the waves as they rolled onto the sand.

Before Communion, there was another water baptism. Linda had asked for this following the healing experience between her and her father the day before. It was good to see her come out of the water so joyous and alive, though I sensed that Len, Linda, and I still had more work to do on our relationships.

Next we gathered in a circle on the beach. Jamie and Charlie had brought a loaf of bread and some juice in a cup; these elements were placed in the middle of our circle. Jamie suggested that this be a different type of Communion, that each one of us should kneel down by the elements and go through a ritual of personal Communion in whatever form seemed appropriate. It could be a prayer, a meditation, a confession, a thanksgiving.

And so we did this, alone, or man and wife together. I was very much moved by the quality of reverence, the depth of repentance, the humility. Virginia Lively was especially affected; she slumped sideways onto the sand from her kneeling position, sobbing her heart out.

Virginia . . . The beauty of the Cape Cod beach, the summer surf pounding against the long, sandy shore, had given us the perfect backdrop for four days and nights of prayer and conversation. As the days passed, and God still did not give me clear direction about whether to share the prophecy He had given me about Amy Catherine, I remained quiet. At least this way I could know my words had no bearing on whether this precious infant lived or died.

Len noticed my silence one evening with a kindly, "Why so quiet, Virginia?"

"Just thoughtful, I guess," I replied.

Over those four days, most of those in our group of sixteen visited Children's Hospital, prayed, pleaded with God. When Amy Catherine got no better, some began to assert, in spite of the evidence, that the miracle was taking place. ("Lord, You are healing her right now!" "We're standing on Your promises, in the name of Jesus!") It seemed almost as if some of these prayer warriors needed to prove to themselves that they had sufficient faith. Did everyone really believe in his or her heart that Amy Catherine was being restored? Or were others, like myself, carrying a silent burden of grief?

My heart ached for the suffering family, while my mind echoed with the words of the prophecy I had received: *This child will not live.* What a contrast with the ringing affirmations of others in the group. The second half of the message, promising health and normalcy to all future offspring of the Marshalls, kept me from feeling completely despondent.

On the final day, in order to celebrate what God had done among us, we had our early morning worship service and Communion on the beautiful expanse of white sand below Rock Harbor Manor. As we walked out to the beach, someone remarked, "Virginia is the only one who hasn't needed ministry!"

Everyone nodded. I had seemed to be the strong one, the one to listen and encourage and pray for the others. Little did they know.

Someone placed the Communion elements, a small loaf of bread and a cup, onto a cloth on the sand. Then we stood in a circle around the elements as Jamie Buckingham led us in worship, offering songs of praise and thanksgiving to God in the soft dawn light.

After Jamie had blessed the elements, each person in turn knelt on the sand and either prayed aloud, meditated silently, or shared an insight. Then each one tore off a piece of the loaf and drank from the cup. Only the breaking of the waves onto the shore and the occasional cry of a seagull punctuated the awe-filled time of remembrance.

As my turn to partake of Communion neared, however, my throat began to ache and tears stung my eyes. Where were they coming from, now of all times? Had they been collecting deep inside without my knowing it, to surface now when I least wanted them to? I didn't even have a handkerchief with me!

As I knelt in the sand, a sob broke my voice. "O Lord," I heard myself cry, "why haven't You healed my daughter?"

What was I saying? I hadn't been thinking that much about Linda—not any more than usual, anyhow. But tears came boiling out as Virginia, the "strong" one who needed no ministry, fell apart before everyone's eyes.

"You promise healing in Your Word, Lord. And I've prayed every way I know how. But You still haven't healed her. It's been so long, and I don't understand. Why don't You do it, Lord? How long do I have to wait?"

My heart felt as though it were splintering and all the pent-up worry and fear of more than a decade pouring out through the cracks. Somehow I had collapsed onto the sand, sobbing like a small, abandoned child.

As I lay there, my own strength exhausted, I was given ears to hear how I sounded: *Why haven't You . . . ? Why don't You . . . ? I don't understand . . . . How long do I have to wait?*

Why, forever, if He chose! I suddenly realized, with stunning clarity, that I didn't have to understand at all! I needed only to come to a point of relinquishment. Never in thirteen years had I really turned Linda's problem over to Him. I had hovered over her fretfully, watched her, nagged her, assuming without ever admitting as much that I could worry and pray at the same time. How many times had I read verses in the Bible without really *hearing* them: "Have no anxiety about anything . . ." (Philippians 4:6) or "Cast all your anxieties on him, for he cares about you" (1 Peter 5:7).

How far I had slipped from that inner awareness that healing is always an unpredictable gift—sheer grace, undeserved favor, nothing I could either work for or earn. His desire to heal and restore, as revealed in Scripture, originated solely because of His goodness and was in keeping with His purpose.

Now I knew what had struck me as familiar in the prayers at Cape Cod for Amy Catherine: they reminded me of my own prayers for my daughter, which had crossed the boundary of expectant faith to the borders of demand!

Something hard inside was melting as I continued to weep in the gathering dawn, surrounded by Christians whom I loved. My attitude and my praying had to change.

"O Lord, You know I love You," I said aloud, struggling back up to my knees. "And Lord, even if You never heal Linda, I'll still love You. I always will. I trust You, Jesus. I leave her in Your hands. Thank You, Lord."

My tears still flowed, but the splintering pain in my heart was lessening. At last I was willing to leave the accomplishment of Linda's healing in the hands of the God who remained sovereign over His creation.

At the close of our bread-breaking service, one of my friends touched my arm and silently handed me a handkerchief. As I turned, I looked into the compassionate eyes of Bob Slosser, who wore the barest hint of a smile. Without a word he opened his arms and enfolded me in them. I felt warm, safe, comforted.

When the group started back to the retreat center for

breakfast—our final meal together before heading to the airport and home—I remained behind for a minute or two, waiting for the sun to slip red above the horizon. Suddenly it emerged, bathing the beach in light, almost as though somebody had flipped on a switch to let the glory of God shine forth.

Binding and Loosing _____

*C*atherine ... Nine of the sixteen prayer partners departed Cape Cod by plane or automobile on Thursday. When we had first gathered in the living room of the Christian Center on Monday morning, we had been a disparate collection of people, with widely different beliefs and lifestyles. A few had been only nominal believers. Many were wrestling with deep personal problems.

In four days we had come together in unity, bonded by intense prayer, tears, and confession. We bid goodbye to the nine with deep emotion, grateful for the healings, but aware that the focus of it all, Amy Catherine, was still untouched.

Surely, Lord, You will not forget this little agent of so much healing.

After Peter and Edith left to spend the evening in their home ten miles away, Scott and Nedra Ross, Linda, Len, and I settled down in that same living room for what I felt would be a relaxed evening. We wanted to seek from Linda gleanings about her future plans, now that she had completed college. By now I realized that Scott and Nedra had been a very positive influence on our daughter and was grateful that they had come.

After we were seated in easy chairs, I asked Linda if she had any plans for the future.

She was silent a moment. "When I arrived here four days ago I had hoped to go to graduate school at Boston University."

"To what purpose?" I asked in some surprise.

"To study counseling at their School of Theology."

"Counseling!" Now I was incredulous. "That seems a bit peculiar, given—"

Len broke in. "Come on, Catherine, let's hear Linda out."

Linda guessed what I had not finished saying. "Mom, I know you think I'm too messed up to be able to help anyone else. Yet my friends—even people I know only casually—come to me with their problems. I'd like my life to count for something significant, and I feel the way to have the greatest impact is with one person at a time. I've gotten disillusioned with trying to change the world through politics or social work."

Though I felt relieved that Linda's political philosophy was changing, I had a sudden *déjà vu* feeling about her wanting to continue her rather aimless and costly education.

But Len was intrigued. "I'm fascinated that you want to be a counselor, Linda. I do think you have a gift for communication and I know you care about people. I'm just not sure you need to go to graduate school at this point. Maybe you should get a job first to find out more about your skills and aptitudes. Possibly do volunteer counseling on the side."

"Definitely," I concurred. "There are better uses for money than graduate school, especially since you haven't applied yourself during college. Forget graduate school, Linda. You need to find a job and earn some money."

Tears filled her eyes. "Why are you always so negative about any plan I come up with, Mom? You keep putting me down."

Len showed his agitation, too. "Catherine, we came here to have a relaxed conversation about Linda's future. You sound like a prosecutor badgering a witness."

Scott and Nedra Ross had been sitting there watching this exchange like spectators at a tennis match. Len turned to them apologetically. "Sorry to make you sit through this family matter."

Nedra shook her head. "Maybe there's a reason for our being here. As an objective listener, I have some insights on your relationships if you're interested."

"Go ahead."

"Each one of you is locked into a position you don't want to be in. Catherine by nature is forthright and pragmatic. Toward her stepdaughter now she is the interrogator, yes. But Catherine has a warm and compassionate side. So why doesn't she show it toward Linda?"

"I'd like the answer to that," said Len.

"Because when Linda finds herself in a shaky position, she has learned that if she gets tearful and plays the role of the 'put-upon' daughter, she wins the sympathy of her father. She almost sets up Catherine to criticize her."

"And Len," Nedra continued, "who is used to being a peacemaker, reacts against the unfairness of strong stepmother tearing into misunderstood stepdaughter. Yet because Len loves you, Catherine, these scenes make him miserable."

"Amen to that," responded Len.

"You, Catherine, don't like it when you find yourself reacting so negatively. And Linda hates playing the divisive role in your family. So all three of you are trapped and unhappy."

"What's the answer?" I asked.

Scott spoke up. "Let me come in at this point. Nedra and I have gotten to know and love Linda this week. She's been very honest with us and I think we have been helpful to her. A lot has happened in her life the last few days. Linda has made a new commitment to the Lord. She and her father had a real breakthrough in their relationship yesterday morning. Now she needs a healing in her relationship with you, Catherine."

"I would like to see that," I replied.

"I really want that, too, Mom," said Linda.

"Good," continued Scott. "The next step might be for Linda to be as open with you two as she was with us. What do you think, Linda?"

Linda nodded. We all sat back in our chairs while she took a deep breath. "Well, first of all. . . ."

She stopped, smiled apologetically, and moved forward in her seat. "What I want to say is this . . . ."

Long pause as Linda put her hand on her throat. A look of bewilderment crossed her face. More resolutely she gripped the side of the chair and started speaking—and stopped again without completing the sentence.

The four of us waited as several more times Linda tried in vain to express herself, each time putting her hand to her throat.

Len offered his daughter reassuring words. Scott and Nedra smiled encouragement. But though her voice sounded fine, Linda could only get out a few syllables.

Half an hour passed. I got up and walked about the room. "You can go to bed if you're tired, Mom." Linda looked relieved at the prospect.

I shook my head. "Linda, I don't know what it is you have

to say to us, but it must be important. So I intend to stay here all night if it's necessary."

"Linda, why do you keep massaging your throat?" Len asked. "Does it hurt?"

Linda shook her head. "No. I just have a funny kind of choking sensation there."

"It may not be funny," suggested Scott. "Let's come against dark powers and principalities right now." Together we prayed for Linda's freedom from any demonic interference.

Another hour went by. I couldn't believe what we were experiencing. "Linda, if you were to tell us at this point that you've had a baby out of wedlock and strangled her, I wouldn't be shocked," I said.

"Oh, Mom, please. It's nothing like that. Must you always expect the absolute worst of me?" She began to cry. But still something was holding her back.

We continued to wait. I placed some pillows on the floor and stretched out on the rug. "If it takes all night, so be it," I said.

Finally, Len had a suggestion. "Linda, maybe the problem is that you're trying to tell us. Why don't you kneel here in front of the couch and say whatever you have to say directly to Jesus. He will free you to talk to Him."

Linda . . . When the five of us gathered together that evening, I felt tied in knots inside. Was it distress over Amy Catherine, uncertainty over my future, the tension I habitually felt when with Mom, or something else entirely?

I was relieved that Scott and Nedra were present. Perhaps they could serve as a buffer between Mom and me, for I was always intimidated by her in these family sessions. I was glad that everyone else was gone, for I had some personal matters to address. I needed to "come clean" with my parents—confess where I had wronged them, ask forgiveness, and begin anew. Yet the early confrontation with Mom threw me off-stride.

How much I had anguished over our relationship. Why was it so unsatisfactory? I longed for that mythical, perfect mother's love, feeling abandoned by my first mother and not really accepted by my second. True, if my performance in school or elsewhere pleased my stepmother, she would be warm and loving to me. If not, I braced myself for criticism. And my behavior *had* left a lot to be desired in recent years, with the chasm between us widening.

Now why couldn't I get the words out? At first it seemed to be the ordinary reluctance one feels in admitting something unpleasant. As time passed, I was embarrassed, frustrated, frightened. How could I do this to my parents and the Rosses? What must they be thinking about me? This session going late into the night was only further exasperating Mom, who greatly prized her rest. Why did I always seem compelled to do the exact opposite of what I should around her, inviting her censure?

When she came out with her worst scenario statement, I was both angry and relieved. For certainly what I had to share wasn't *that* bad! And Nedra had said kindly, "Linda, even if that were true, it's not too big for God. There's *nothing* He can't or won't forgive."

When Dad suggested I get on my knees and talk to Jesus, the release came. Up until then, I'd been trying to confess to the other people in the room, afraid of what they'd think of me, fearful of further rejection. Now I was able to put those fears and my desire for approval aside. Haltingly at first, then in a torrent, I poured out my heart to the Lord. As I confessed my rebelliousness and irresponsibility, my tears no longer stemmed from my own pain—I began to grieve over how I had sinned against God Himself.

In the ensuing quiet, I began to sense the inner peace and freedom I had been longing for. Then I rose, turned to my

parents, and asked their forgiveness. It wasn't an emotional
scene. In fact, it was curiously matter-of-fact. There were
embraces all around and goodnights exchanged with dis-
patch.

As I lay in bed that night I felt stripped and drained.
There was no exhilaration but I didn't mind that. I knew the
Christian walk wasn't based on feelings but obedience.
Now I had done my part and I was in God's hands.

When I sat down to breakfast with Mom the next morning, I noticed that she had brought her Bible with her, which
was unusual. I was curious as to how she would treat me,
but I felt an odd new sense of detachment.

"Linda," she began, "I'm sure you recall the story of the
Prodigal Son."

I nodded, for I had expected the comparison.

She opened her Bible and asked me to read that wonderful story from Luke 15:11–31. When I finished she looked
at me and said: "I have a confession of my own to make,
Linda. When you received God's all-restoring forgiveness
last night, my reaction was: All those years of anxiety and
turmoil you put your father and me through, and now
you're forgiven by God *instantly*. Isn't that too easy?

"Well, this morning I received my answer. I was awakened to a clear, incisive, internal message: 'Remember My
story of the Prodigal Son? Catherine, you're in grave danger
of taking the place of the elder brother in that drama. *Let all
negative thoughts about Linda go as of this moment*. As of
now you are to take the lowest seat at My banquet table,
below Len, below Linda. And you are to confess all this to
her this morning.' "

There was an odd uncertainty in Mom's face as she continued. "So, as your brothers would say, I have been properly zapped. Linda, will you forgive me?"

Again I was at a loss for words, this time overwhelmed by
the wonder of it all. The awareness that the Lord God

Himself loved, accepted, and forgave me began to bubble up inside. God cared enough about me to "zap" my famous and celebrated stepmother! He really did love me!

"Oh, Mom, I'm blown away. Of course I forgive you. But there's something else." I struggled to give words to my thoughts. "I think I went farther than you realize in blaming myself for the things that have gone wrong—Eve's alcoholism, my schoolwork, the problems you and Dad have had. Even though I believed in God all those years, I always felt He was in your corner—so I doubted He could really be in mine.

"What you've said to me this morning means more to me than you'll ever know. For in spite of all the misunderstandings and hurt, you've always been extremely important to me." My voice caught. Awkwardly we got up and embraced.

"Oh, Mom, I really love you."

"And I love you, Linda."

This time I cried from pure joy. If Mom, who always seemed so close to God, wasn't mad at me, God probably wasn't either! Perhaps He even had good things in store for me.

Black Friday _____

*C*atherine ... Our intense prayer time at Rock Harbor Manor ended on August 12. Len and I stayed another two days on the Cape, then drove to Boston to spend a day at Children's Hospital before heading back to our summer base at Evergreen Farm in Virginia. We'd been told that Amy Catherine's condition had stabilized and I took this as a sign that our prayers had begun to make a difference, that the healing had begun.

When we arrived at the hospital, we discovered that Amy Catherine had been moved to Division 20, which is Clinical Research. A slim young Filipino nurse greeted us and took us into a room where there were two large glittering steel cribs.

I had a sinking feeling that this was the wrong place for Amy Catherine, that she belonged in a much smaller, cozier crib. This room seemed cold, stark. I picked up the tiny baby and held her in my arms. Then I sat down and began to love her.

Len and I both saw changes for the better in Amy Catherine. She was more active. She moved her hand to her face, a perfectly normal baby gesture. Then she began to cry. I concluded that Amy Catherine had gotten accustomed to being fed every time she was picked up. The fact that she kept turning toward my breast and opening her little mouth like a baby bird really got to me.

I looked her over carefully. The lovely pink face with the rosebud mouth reminded me of Mary Elizabeth. Both were such beautiful children. Only Amy Catherine's eyes weren't quite right.

The nurse came in and began feeding Amy Catherine from a bottle. It took a long time, about an hour, to get a few ounces of milk down her. Len and I walked about the hospital, stopping as always in the chapel. The stained glass window with a picture of a nurse and a child was somehow comforting.

As Len and I sat on the wooden bench meditating, my mind drifted back over the past week. So many lives touched. It was as though each person who came to pray for Amy Catherine received a blessing. Linda, most spectacularly. She was now on her way back to Maine to finish her summer stint at her grandmother's gift shop. *Lord, I pray You will guide her into a productive new life.*

I thanked God for the healing between myself and the Sherrills. For the way the Holy Spirit had moved in Peter's life, in Edith's, in Jamie's, in Len's, in Pam's, in Scott Ross', in Virginia's. And probably in all the others, too, in ways I didn't know at that time.

You were there, Lord! And You are here now healing Amy Catherine! Thank You, Lord!

Late that afternoon Len and I drove to New York City so that Len could catch up on his work at the office. I was most reluctant to leave Boston because in my heart I felt a continuous prayer ministry was needed at Amy Catherine's bedside. The medical personnel there felt her situation was hopeless, and though cooperative with our requests in every way, I feared that their unbelief in supernatural healing could impede the Spirit's ministrations.

What the doctors really wanted to do was perform certain tests on the baby, including a liver biopsy. I had urged Peter and Edith not to consent to this. I felt I had received specific guidance from the Lord that snipping out a piece of Amy Catherine's liver would traumatize her and undo the progress she had made. To my alarm, Peter and Edith had allowed the doctors to persuade them to agree to the biopsy. Then at the last moment the doctors themselves canceled the operation because they felt the baby was too weak.

This was the status of things at the hospital when Len and I left New York to continue on to Evergreen Farm where my mother was expecting us. Since Peter had a canoe trip with the youth of his church scheduled long beforehand for the end of August, Edith and Mary Elizabeth joined us at the farm for the week that Peter was gone. For the first time since the baby's birth a month earlier, Edith was able to relax for a few days.

I found myself struggling again with the passage in Daniel that Peter had been given a few days after Amy Catherine's birth:

> . . . In the midst of the week he shall cause the sacrifice and the oblation to cease, and for the overspreading of abominations he shall make it desolate. . . .

How did this relate to Amy Catherine? I looked it up in the Interpreter's Bible and got little help. It seemed to allude to some kind of decree by Antiochus of Syria that suspended sacrifice and offerings for a period of three-and-a-half years. In their place would be offered the abomination of heathen sacrifice.

A footnote, however, grabbed my attention: "The abomination ... is the idol set up in the temple—a common theme throughout the Bible. Idols have a terrible fascination for men [who] want to put something of their own creation in the place of God. This is a clue to the whole tragedy of humanity."

A thought began to germinate in my mind. What was the Lord trying to say to Peter through this verse? Was He saying that men (including Peter) are distracted by things like work and sports, which become idols and keep men from a closer relationship to Him?

Nothing particularly new about this. Men have always made idols of their cars, their sports ability, their work skills, their sexual prowess, and so on. Was the Lord trying to warn Peter of something here? The canoe trip, for example? In view of Amy Catherine's condition I questioned Peter about taking such a trip, when he would be out of communication with us for days. He considered canceling it at one point; then, when the baby's condition stabilized, he decided not to disappoint the young people in his church.

Friday, August 27, at Evergreen Farm began with a call by Edith to Children's Hospital. She talked to the doctor who told her, "Your baby has responded so well to blood transfusions that we're going ahead with the liver biopsy."

When Edith reported this to us at breakfast, my heart sank. I begged Edith to call the doctor back and ask him to cancel the surgery. Edith refused to do this. When the four of us—Mother, Edith, Len, and myself—gathered in the living room to pray about it, I found myself in a difficult situation. Both Mother and Edith had always placed doctors on a pedestal, were too quick, in my opinion, to accept their verdicts and opinions as gospel. Len was neutral, again inclined to play the role of peacemaker. He certainly did not share my strong conviction about the biopsy. I sensed, too, that he was resistant to what he felt was my "slugger" approach.

I confess that I handled this confrontation badly. Instead of simply reiterating what I believed I had received from the Lord, that the biopsy should be avoided at all costs, I bore into Edith.

"Since Peter is on a canoe trip, Edith, you're the only one who can stop this awful procedure."

"I'm sorry, Mom, but I don't feel I'm supposed to do that. Peter and I together gave them the okay. I have no new reason for asking them to stop it."

"You have a very good reason. It will do great harm to your baby."

"The doctors don't feel that way. They say it's only a minor procedure."

"Edith, cutting out a piece of a baby's liver is not minor. The doctors have given up on Amy Catherine. They're only interested in her for medical research. As the mother, how can you let your own flesh and blood go through this unnecessary operation?"

Tears of anguish formed in Edith's eyes and I calmed down a bit. "What time is the biopsy to be done?" I asked.

"Early this afternoon."

"Would you do this? Would you call the doctor and ask him to postpone the biopsy until Peter returns from his canoe trip and the two of you can review the situation?"

Edith turned to my mother and Len. "What do you think I should do?"

As I expected Mother sided with Edith. "If you and Peter

prayed it through, and then decided to allow the biopsy, it must be right."

Len put the cap on it. "Peter as the spiritual head of his household gave the go-ahead for this biopsy. I can understand why Edith is reluctant to change that decision."

I was furious with my husband.

We stopped talking at this point and prayed together. The substance of the prayers: "We turn this situation over to You, Lord. If You do not want the biopsy to take place, we know You will stop it as You did before."

Later that day northern Virginia was hit by violent thunderstorms, rain, and hail. The wind tore down several trees on the farm; we lost our electricity for a while.

Completely appropriate, I thought to myself. This is *Black Friday* in every way. That evening I went upstairs to our room, lay down on the bed, and sobbed and sobbed.

On Saturday, August 28, I awoke in an agony of spirit. During our early morning prayer time together Len was tender but firm with me. I had overstepped my position. I was the grandmother, not the mother of Amy Catherine, so owed Edith an apology for my overbearing attitude. And I needed to act quickly since Edith and Mary Catherine were taking the noon plane back to Boston.

It was difficult for me to apologize because my guidance about the biopsy was so clear. When I knocked on Edith's door, she answered sleepily and invited me inside. I sat on her bed and asked her to forgive me for the way I handled the situation. We both wept, then hugged each other.

The call came from Edith the following day, Sunday afternoon. "Amy Catherine is in critical condition. She has jaundice and seizures. Her body is on a machine." She began to sob.

"I'll check with Len," I told her. "If he's free we'll both fly up to Boston tomorrow morning. We'll take a cab from the airport and meet you at the hospital."

As I hung up the thought struck me: *I was right about the biopsy. But being right may be a bigger burden to carry than if I had been wrong.*

Len was able to switch some dates so we both took the morning flight. Edith met us in the lobby of the Children's Inn, an accommodation for families of patients. We registered, then walked over to the hospital together. Peter was driving up from the Cape and would join us later in the day.

When Edith and I walked into Amy Catherine's room, my heart broke. Her naked little form had been placed on a tilted heat bed in the middle of the room. Over it was a small canopy with a lamp from which the heat flowed. On a table nearby the heart monitor gave a steady *beep beep beep.* Wires seemed to be attached to every part of her body: one to record the heartbeat, one for her breathing, one as a catheter, a tube in her foot for intravenous feeding. Another tube ran down her nose into her stomach.

Edith was crying and my own chest was heaving with sobs. The whole scene was so grim: aside from the tilted bed, there was a bulletin board on the wall filled with notices, a washbasin for the nurses and doctors, a nurse's table, a few chairs, a linoleum floor, and all these machines. The room was coldly sterile in every way.

When Edith left to make some phone calls, I was alone with the baby for several minutes. I studied Amy Catherine. She was a pasty yellow color from the jaundice. I wanted so much to hold her. The nurse entered and proceeded to bathe the tiny infant within and around the life-support paraphernalia. At first she seemed disconcerted that I was there watching her. Then as she finished she said impulsively, "You know, I don't see any reason why you couldn't *hold* Amy Catherine."

"I would certainly like to do that," I replied, wondering

how I could pick Amy Catherine up with all these wires and tubes protruding from her.

The nurse gave me a white gown to put on and instructed me to sit down close to the tile-bed so that nothing had to be disconnected. My hands were trembling as I lifted her onto my lap.

The moment I touched Amy Catherine it was as if the stench of death left the room. Her eyelids fluttered; gurgling noises came out of her mouth; she moved her hands about as if she wanted to touch back.

Edith soon joined me and we took turns holding Amy Catherine, clucking and exclaiming over every nuance in her response to us. Our need at that point was to pour out love to this helpless and internally damaged child.

The realization soon hit us that the simple fact of being held and cuddled was making a difference to her physically. Even the doctors and the nurses began commenting on how well she was responding. Clutching at hope we decided to continue this kind of treatment night and day between Peter, Edith, Len, me, and others who came to visit and pray for her.

That night Len and I spent a long time praying in the hospital chapel before going to bed. In the morning I awoke with a Scripture passage in my mind about the paralytic man let down through the roof by his four friends: "Jesus *seeing their faith* healed him" (Mark 2:5).

It was as if I had received a thunderous answer from God the Father Himself: that disbelief in God's goodness is the worst sin of all. Not only is it God's will to heal, but for us to believe that He desires anything else saddens Him more than any sex sin. The way He wants us to deal with unbelief is exactly the way we deal with any other sin: bring it to the foot of the cross, confess it, ask forgiveness and cleansing, and receive back faith as a gift.

Over and over in the Gospels Jesus stresses the all-importance of faith. "Go, and it shall be done for you *as you have believed*" (Matthew 8:13). Or in the case of the woman with the issue of blood: "It's *your faith* that has made you well" (Mark 5:34). To the two blind men: "Do you really *believe* that I can do this for you?" And when they answered in the affirmative, then: "According to *your faith* be it unto you" (Matthew 9:28–29).

Most definitive of all was the statement He made to His disciples when they had been unable to heal the demoniac boy. "Why weren't we able to do this?" they asked Him. And He answered clearly and unequivocally, "*Because of your little faith*" (Matthew 17:19–20).

Above all other qualities, Jesus calls us to faith. Furthermore, He tells us that the *difficulty* of the situation has nothing at all to do with its solution. He says that there is never any doubt about whether He is *able* to handle any situation. The only question mark points to *me* and my faith in Him. Jesus tells us: "*Everything* is possible for one who has faith" (Mark 9:23).

Thus my question "Is it really God's will to heal today?" was answered. Here I had been trying since Sunday to relinquish Amy Catherine, while Jesus seemed to be saying, "Sorry, that would be far too easy. The minute you turn your back on the situation, and don't count any unbelief in you as the sin it is, you are also turning your back on the living God."

My faith was rejuvenated.

During the second day of our holding Amy Catherine, she showed decided improvement. Her heart was so much stronger that the doctor decided there was no need to monitor it every minute. The heart machine was just turned off. Silently Edith and I cheered.

The next two days we were in and out of Amy Catherine's room at all hours, having some rather strange yet cozy times with her and with the night nurses who weren't used to all this company. During this time Edith really got to know her baby as she cuddled and mothered her. The atmosphere in the room became noticeably cheerier, and from a tiny, wired-up patient, Amy Catherine turned into an individual. It was during these days that the baby got to me totally.

Walking on Water _____

*C*atherine . . . Linda returned from Maine on August 30 and settled in the Marshall home in East Dennis to help care for Mary Elizabeth and free Peter and Edith to spend more time at the hospital. By now there was a steady procession of visitors, mostly from Peter's church, to help with our prayer vigil. When Len had to return to Florida to help our two sons get off to school, I stayed alone at the Children's Inn, going back and forth from my room to the hospital.

Two couples from the Boston area heard that Peter Marshall's granddaughter was critically ill at Children's Hospital and came to visit one night when I was there alone. People from Rock Harbor Manor agreed to come during the night so that Edith and I could sleep while prayer continued 'round the clock.

The hospital personnel were cooperative and friendly, if a bit incredulous at our tenacity. An English physician, in this country on some kind of exchange arrangement, was in charge of the case. As he bent over the crib to peer closely at Amy Catherine, with his full beard almost tickling her stomach, he seemed like something out of a Dickens novel.

Once after examining the baby, he turned to me and asked in a pleasant voice, "Will you be going on holiday on the Cape this weekend?"

I shook my head. "Until Amy Catherine gets better, I'll be here."

He seemed puzzled. "There's really nothing you can do for her."

My response: "As long as there is breath in Amy Catherine's body, I'll be here to pray for her."

To the doctor and the nurses coming in and out of the room I must have seemed like a complete fanatic. I'm sure I was, during the whole six weeks that had now elapsed since Amy Catherine's birth. It was an all-out faith walk on my part, the most exhilarating experience of my life. If you talk about adventure, there is no adventure like totally trusting God. It was like spending six weeks walking on the water, or parachuting out of a plane, or climbing Mt. Everest.

The closest comparable experience was just after Peter Marshall's death when I was living in the Kingdom of God on earth and knew with great sureness what I was to do each moment. This was different in that we were walking in blind faith. We really were. I mean there was no *sight* in it— literally no way to see what lay before us. Perhaps it wasn't a faith walk at all, and we were running far ahead of the Lord. But at the time we felt we were being obedient. The highs were thrilling, the lows devastating.

One such low came Friday night, September 3. Amy

Catherine had had a restless day. One of the nurses had seemed so callous and brusque that I asked another nurse what was wrong. "She's going through a divorce," she replied.

The baby's body seemed more jaundiced than usual. Again I agonized over the damage the liver biopsy had done to her. What had it accomplished, really? From my room at Children's Inn I called Sandra Ghost, one of my Florida prayer partners and a woman who was going through a faith walk with her own child. She had a specific word for me: *I was to raise my eyes from the immediate situation in the hospital room and see the heavenly hosts struggling to help us.*

She called my attention to a passage in the Old Testament where help was slow in reaching the prophet Daniel. Eventually an archangel appeared to Daniel and told him that he'd been delayed "in the heavenlies" 21 days, fighting evil forces in the spiritual universe in order to battle his way through to earth (Daniel 10:12).

The next morning, Saturday, September 4, I was up early and reread this chapter of Daniel. Whenever we ask for a miracle, apparently, we can expect to engage in this kind of spiritual warfare. *Lord, help me to continue to be strong in battle,* I prayed. Once more I marveled over how I was able to overcome my usual limitations of shortness of breath, lack of energy, early fatigue—all surmounted in my total concentration on the baby.

How have I managed this, Lord? I'd spent long hours of prayer, watching and ministering there in the hospital, day after day after day, and well into the night. I just didn't have this kind of vitality. *Are You giving it to me, Lord?* I know that Len and others think I'm doing this not only because Amy Catherine is my grandchild, my flesh and blood, but because she bears my name. There may be something to this, Lord. I've always been a battler for what I felt was right. You gave me this competitive quality and I've had to use it in life over and over again. Now I see this same quality in Amy Catherine. I see it in her now as she fights for life against all the odds. All my own determination and drive reach out to this child to establish contact with the fighting spirit in her. I'm saying to her, "You'll make it and I'll fight with you. Two Catherines slugging it out together."

Edith joined me at the hospital Saturday morning. Again we took turns holding Amy Catherine, cooing to her, loving her. She was not responding as well as she had earlier in the week. Her color was bad and the heart monitor had been reattached.

Because Amy Catherine had not taken the bottle very well after the biopsy operation, the doctor had been feeding glucose to her through the tube in her nose. A few ounces of glucose were given to her this way every couple of hours, after which they had to pump the bile out of her stomach through another tube.

The mid-morning feeding went routinely. But when they began pumping the bile out of her stomach, Amy Catherine protested with cries and whimpers. I was sitting by her crib at the time, my stomach protesting, too.

After the second feeding several hours later, Amy Catherine was put into my arms while the nurse began pumping out the bile. This time Amy Catherine began crying loudly. She didn't like it at all and was telling us so.

The nurse kept on pumping and would not stop even when I urged her to. Suddenly her eyes darted to the heartbeat machine. The rhythm had slowed. "I think we'd better put her back in the crib," she said, then went running for the doctor.

The doctor and Edith, who had gone for snacks, arrived at the same moment. When she looked at the baby, Edith exclaimed, "Something's wrong! Why is her skin so mottled?"

The doctor bent over Amy Catherine for several minutes then looked up and said gently, "The baby has expired. I'm sorry." I will never forget that he used the word expired.

Edith began to cry. Somehow I could not. The time was 2:18 P.M. How strange that I remember this fact!

I went over to the crib, placed my hand on the baby's head, and quite blatantly asked God to restore her to life. Somehow I was not willing to believe that it was going to end like this. I kept my hands on her for quite some time. Her little head was turned slightly to one side away from me. She still had no clothes on. Her mouth was so much like Mary Elizabeth's—the one thing that I had noticed over and over during these weeks. Perhaps from the heat above, her body was still perfectly warm. But, oh, so quiet.

I checked out of the Children's Inn, eager now to get away from the scene of so much pain. Edith and I were silent during the drive to the Cape.

That night I stayed with Mary Elizabeth while Peter, Edith, and Linda went over to the church to the Upper Room Fellowship. It was a very hot night and Mary Elizabeth was restless, so I went up to her room and sat down in a chair by her crib. Somehow I was able to relate to this child whereas I had been silent during the grown-up conversation at dinner.

We sang some songs and talked. Mary Elizabeth kept pushing her stuffed animals and her dolls through the bars of the crib until my whole lap was covered with them. And so a two-and-a-half-year-old ministered to me in a way no adult could have.

Searching for Reasons _____

*C*atherine ... Peter's church had an overflow congregation the following day, Sunday, September 5. In fact, Peter had had overflow congregations all summer long, for the drama of a tiny infant's fight for life had gotten to many people on the Cape.

I was in such a state of depression that I have little recollection of that service. It was an especially difficult assignment for Peter, the bereaved father, to try to explain to his church why God would take this precious child when Peter didn't understand it himself. It was especially awkward for him since he had gone all-out for a supernatural healing.

Peter did the best he could. In essence, he took the blame upon himself, which may have been right for him to do as head of his home, but which left many with theological questions.

I certainly had questions. What had made me so certain that God was going to heal Amy Catherine? Like Peter, I had gone out on a limb in this regard. Had God told me He was going to heal the baby? I certainly thought He had. There were several occasions when I had felt His assurance about this. Obviously I had been wrong and, yes, I was angry about it. And I was still deeply upset with Peter and Edith about the biopsy.

The thought settled on me that but for the biopsy Amy Catherine would have made it. God's plan for Amy Catherine was thwarted by the disobedience of His children. How often that had happened in the history of mankind!

The rehashing of our words and actions began on Monday night at 6 P.M. in Peter and Edith's living room. Len was still in Florida but was flying to Washington the next day to meet us there for the burial service at Fort Lincoln Cemetery, where Peter Marshall and Peter Christopher had also been laid to rest. Linda was at the Marshalls' along with another couple. The six of us planned to go out for dinner.

Something was said to the effect that we had "missed it" with Amy Catherine and we were off. It would be almost 10 P.M., four hours later, before we would think about food. At the beginning a lot of anger, resentment, and pain came out. I admitted my sense of defeat. "I have never given myself so completely to anything in life as I did to Amy Catherine. When Peter Marshall died, painful as it was, I felt God's presence in the hospital room. Not with Amy Catherine's death. It was as if God had left us, too, along with the baby."

Then Linda spoke up. "I've been doing a lot of praying the last few nights. Would you all be interested in what I feel God has been saying to me?"

A bit self-consciously she read from a yellow pad some of

her journal entries, concluding with this passage from Scripture:

> "My thoughts are not your thoughts, neither are your ways My ways," declares the Lord. "For as the heavens are higher than the earth, so are My ways higher than your ways, and My thoughts than your thoughts."
>
> Isaiah 55-8–9, NIV

"Maybe," Linda concluded, "we're not supposed to understand all that God was doing through Amy Catherine. He certainly touched a lot of lives."

"That's true," Peter responded. "Yet I sensed that the sixteen of us were not in unity in our prayers for her."

"What you're saying, Peter," I said, "is that we failed, not God. How do you feel that you failed?"

Peter shifted about uncomfortably on the floor where he was sitting. "I should never have gone on that canoe trip. It was all wrong." Suddenly he began sobbing. "I simply did not care enough to give everything to the baby."

For a moment I was back in our home in 1949 at the moment I received the telephone call telling me of Peter Marshall's death in George Washington University Hospital. When Peter, age nine, had cried then, I had taken him in my arms. Now I moved over beside him and put my arms about him.

Edith's turn was next. Haltingly and painfully she confessed that throughout the six weeks of Amy's life she had harbored a hidden fear that God would not heal the baby in spite of our fervent prayers. She suspected that her faithlessness was rooted in past experience. After all, her own mother had died when she was a little girl; then Peter Christopher. With sobs, she broke down. "I just don't know what He wants of us! What kind of God is He, anyway?"

It was a powerful time of honesty and ministry one to

another. The evening ended on a single note: *It was not God
who had failed, but we who had failed.*

The funeral at Peter's church the next morning stressed
this same theme. I spoke briefly at the service. "When you
go all-out to claim one of the promises in Scripture," I said,
"and the baby dies, this can be devastating to your faith.
Yesterday I was prepared to resign as a roving editor for
Guideposts and tell McGraw-Hill that I would be doing no
further books on religious subjects. But as we prayed and
shared together last night in the Marshall home, it became
so clear to us. God hadn't failed us. He had a plan for the
healing of Amy Catherine. Through our disobedience we
thwarted His plan."

After the funeral, Peter, Edith, and I drove to Hyannis
Airport and boarded a small private plane for the flight to
Washington, D.C. In the baggage section of the plane, beside
our luggage, was Amy Catherine's tiny coffin.

The burial service at Fort Lincoln Cemetery was a simple
one. Len joined us there, along with my brother, Bob, my
sister, Emma Lynn, and their families, plus a few close
friends. Peter's message was much the same as he'd given in
East Dennis earlier that day, identifying our lack of faith and
unity as the hindrance to God's perfect plan. I wept only
when I saw Amy Catherine Marshall's little coffin about to
take its place beside the equally tiny coffin of Peter Christopher Marshall.

Afterward Bob and Len were talking about Peter's burial
message and I overheard Bob say, "We certainly have a bigger God than *that*, don't we?" That statement troubled me.

The next day Len and I flew back to our home in Florida.
In the evening I placed a call to my friend Sandra Ghost
whose gifts of wisdom and discernment had been so helpful to me during this crisis. I told her about the repentance
time Monday night and our conclusion that we, not God,
had failed.

Sandra was silent for a long moment after my report. Then she said, "Catherine, that seems to imply a huge emphasis on works, as though the healing depended upon man. God's grace is much greater than all that, isn't it?"

By the time I hung up the phone, the heaviness had returned to my spirit. I turned to Len and remarked, "I sure wish I hadn't called Sandra tonight."

Somehow I wasn't ready to consider the question both Bob and Sandra had raised.

Virginia Lively . . . One of the hardest things I've ever done in my life was to go to Catherine and share the prophetic word I'd had about Amy Catherine: "This child will not live. But any other child they have they may have in perfect confidence." Several days after Catherine's return to Florida I made a date to see her at her Boynton Beach home.

When I arrived I could tell that Catherine was despondent. "I've had trouble sleeping," she confided. "My mind keeps going back to Children's Hospital. There on the heat bed is that helpless, dear little baby with all those tubes sticking out of her. I just start weeping." Her eyes filled as she spoke.

We reminisced for a while as I tried to summon the courage to confess what I had withheld from her and the others at Cape Cod. Finally, it came out: the prophecy about Amy Catherine.

Catherine blinked as though I'd struck her in the face. Moments of silence.

"Why . . . why . . . why, Virginia, did you keep silent? It would have made all the difference."

"But would it have really?" I replied. "I don't think you would have accepted it. And there would have been a negative pall over the whole week, interfering perhaps with all the good things that did happen. When the baby died I would always have wondered if my nay-saying had affected the outcome. Can you see my position, Catherine?"

Catherine nodded, but I knew her well enough to tell she was deeply angry. There was darkness in her spirit. Intense misery. It frightened me. I loved her so.

We talked about other things, awkwardly. Catherine could not, would not bring up again the subject of Amy Catherine. Driving back to my home in Belle Glade, I reviewed the situation for the thousandth time.

Would my talking to her earlier have prepared her for Amy Catherine's death, and alleviated her depression to some degree? Would it have brought on the depression sooner? Would it have antagonized her, since it flew in the face of what she believed she had heard? Should I have spoken up anyway and let the chips fall where they might, letting the Lord handle the problem? Or was it right, what I did do—hide it in my heart, using it as personal information only, until receiving a further word from God?

So disturbed was I that I shared my concern with Freddie Koch, a close friend of Catherine's and mine. Freddie was troubled about a vivid dream she had just had, resulting, she felt, from her prayers for Catherine. We decided we should share the dream with both Catherine and Len.

The four of us gathered together in Boynton Beach and Freddie described her dream. It seemed that Freddie was trying to get to Amy Catherine in the hospital and was having a very hard time doing this because nurses and doctors kept stopping her. But Freddie felt that she simply had to get to the baby's side and pray for her. Finally Freddie did reach Amy Catherine, but, instead of praying for her, she found herself coping with the remnant of a very dirty diaper.

The rest of the dream involved the details of cleaning up the messy diaper, disposing of it, and so forth. Freddie never did get back to Amy Catherine to minister to her. And there the dream ended.

The vividness of the imagery startled us. My interpretation of it was: "The Lord is trying to tell us that we are spending a great amount of time trying to deal with something that the baby has finished with, gotten rid of. What I see is that Amy Catherine is with Jesus. What we are doing here, in our human way, is dealing with all the after-effects of the experience, the residue of the whole affair. We are spending a lot of energy on this residue, trying to decide about where to put everything, trying to find neat solutions to it all, and this is not what the Lord asks of us at all. *He is saying that the baby is with Him and that we are to forget all the why-this and why-that and get on with worshiping the Lord and praising Him for the way that Amy Catherine ministered to so many people while on earth.*"

Catherine, I could tell, was not satisfied with that interpretation of this dream. On the contrary, she felt that the dirty diaper represented the mess, the impurities, the sin in our lives, and that the mess was so big that we never did get around to praying effectively for Amy Catherine. The reason the baby died was that there wasn't enough prayer power, that we weren't clean enough channels through whom God could work.

Catherine seemed determined to see man's failure as the culprit; nothing Freddie and I could say could convince her otherwise. My heart ached for Catherine. She was having trouble praying. There was deep hurt in her voice. I think she felt that God had betrayed her, that in a smaller way I, too, had betrayed her. *O Lord,* I pleaded, *be tender with her.*

Peter . . . After Amy's burial in Fort Lincoln Cemetery, Edith and I stayed on in Virginia for a much-needed recuperation period at Evergreen Farm. But although there was physical rest, there was no rest for our souls, for we were spiritually depressed and defeated. Amy was dead; we had blown it. I was burdened by the thought that it was somehow all our fault.

It was only when Edith and I got back to Cape Cod, and I resumed my life and ministry at the East Dennis Church, that the bigger picture of Amy's life and death began to come into focus. I saw that I had fallen into the trap of believing that if we could just muster enough faith, God would have healed Amy.

I knew better than this. As a pastor I had walked through deaths with people whose healings had been prayed for with utmost faith; I knew perfectly well that human failure was not to blame.

The New Testament is full of Jesus' healings, but He didn't heal everybody, every time. At the pool of Bethesda where Jesus healed a cripple, the healed man walked out of the place past all the prone bodies of the other invalids.

Eventually, these truths emerged from the birth, brief life, and death of our little girl. Our God is the sovereign Lord of life and death; our times and seasons are truly in His hands. Healing is truly a divine mystery, and God has His inscrutable purposes for each person's life. The healing power of Jesus is not a supernatural power source that can be tapped into by a special group of Christians who learn the secret formulas of faith. The Lord of the universe will be controlled by no man's faith. God is never under man's influence; He is always free. Healing remains in the hands of the One who triumphed over man's sin and sicknesses on the cross . . . yet it is often His good pleasure to express His healing love through the prayers and ministry of His servants. But not every time and not solely in response to our initiative. Sometimes our God has plans and designs for people's lives that we cannot possibly fathom.

Had I lost my faith in divine healing? Only temporarily, until I realized that Amy's death had not resulted from a lack of faith. In the weeks following Amy's death I found that I believed in spiritual healing as much as ever, for I had learned that our faith is not to be in healing, but in the God who heals!

I believe that Mother knew all this, too. She was simply blinded for a while by her intense involvement with our baby. I can understand that; most of the sixteen of us who met on the Cape lost our perspective, too, during those incredible days. Though Amy Catherine's death was the immediate trigger, I believe it was the combination of things going wrong in her life that brought on Mother's time of darkness.

Section III
The Dark Night
of the Soul

"Are you in the dark just now in your circumstances, or in your life with God? Then remain quiet. If you open your mouth in the dark, you will talk in the wrong mood: darkness is the time to listen."

Oswald Chambers

Editor's Note ... I suspect that if Catherine had been assured by the Lord that it was lack of unity of the sixteen and disobedience by Peter and Edith that prevented Him from healing Amy Catherine, she would have accepted that. That would have been human failure, and Catherine was never surprised at human failure. Her sorrow would probably have lifted fairly quickly. When she learned of Virginia Lively's foreknowledge about the baby's death, however, directly opposite to the word she felt she had received from God, Catherine was devastated. She had gone all-out in faith and felt that God had let her down. In addition she felt humiliated in front of family and friends: Virginia had heard God correctly, she herself had not.

At this point Catherine entered a period of darkness. Her regular journal entries for the next six months virtually ceased. The following section is pieced together from notations she made to herself, her letters to family and friends, some dreams she recorded, and my own memories of conversations and confrontations we had. She stayed angry at God for many weeks; then when she sought to renew the relationship there was nothing. Only silence—and darkness.

The Clouds Descend _____

Catherine ... I believe that Satan won the victory last summer in the Amy Catherine situation. His handwork is all through it.

As I told the family the night before the funeral, there was a vast difference between the day of Amy Catherine's death and that of Peter Marshall back in 1949. I felt Jesus' presence in the room where Peter died. For a week after his death I walked in the glory of the Kingdom of God on earth.

At the time of Amy Catherine's death I could not feel Jesus' presence in her hospital room. On the contrary, I sensed evil there. We did not walk in any glory in the days following. Far from it! There was dissension, blame flung about, nitpicking over various decisions, a sense of failure.

Despite the good things that happened to some of the people who gathered to pray on Cape Cod, I have seen no good come from Amy Catherine's death itself. Only misunderstanding and confusion. I have not understood why the results were so negative. I have not understood what was behind all this.

Could Amy Catherine's genetically damaged body somehow have been demon-possessed? If so, was it wrong to anoint her with oil and claim a healing? Would a completely different kind of deliverance prayer have worked the miracle?

But *how* could we have gone ahead with an exorcism over an innocent newborn child without a specific revelation from God?

I dreamed last night that I was in my own home, though it was a larger house than our actual one, with several floors. Climbing to the top floor I found to my surprise six people living there. They were not overtly antagonistic toward me, but were obviously intruders; they had moved in secretly and were doing their housekeeping with inadequate equipment, a scruffy broom, etc.

Today in trying to interpret this dream, I sought the identity of my "squatters" so that they could be ousted. The first appeared to be "depression," the second "unshed tears," the third "grief." That's all I've gotten so far.

The fourth one of the "squatters" in my dream of several days ago has to be "sleeplessness." On the way to the airport to fly to New York yesterday, I realized that I had left my sleeping pills behind. So last night in the New York hotel I did my usual lying there, hour after hour, waiting for dawn. Just a bit of dozing the last few hours. Then I awoke with a raging headache. And still no feeling of Jesus' presence at all.

Yesterday I was struck by a phrase I read somewhere long ago: *We learn humility through humiliations.*

Having gone through a humiliation last summer, I should have much more humility today. Yet I don't feel that I've grown spiritually in this area. I don't feel that I've grown spiritually in any area these past months.

Humiliation. The dictionary calls it "a painful loss of pride, dignity, and self-respect." I feel I represent every bit of that description and I don't like it at all.

My humiliation, of course, is a paltry nothing compared to the humiliation suffered by Jesus on the cross. Yet somehow Jesus and His suffering seem remote, unconnected with me and my present misery—that's all I seem to think about these days. I'm aware of a fatal self-centeredness here, but seem incapable of breaking free.

I woke up this morning with a Scripture passage running through my head: *No one is able to come to me unless he [or she] is drawn by the Father* (John 6:44, MOFFATT).

"Does that mean," I asked myself, "that I can't have a relationship with Jesus unless God instigates it?"

My mind whirled back through the years. Had God drawn me to Jesus as a child? Obviously so. The Father in heaven had drawn me to the Son. But now I feel no relationship with either Jesus or the Father. It seemed to end the day Amy Catherine died. So the Father must be blocking me from this relationship. Why?

I don't want to pursue it further. It's too painful. The hurt over my grandchild's death has to heal. I'm incapable of seeking understanding by going back over the events yet again.

So where does this leave me? Wallowing in my sin? Clearly this is so, but I feel helpless to do anything about it. I'm reminded bitterly of an article I wrote for *Guideposts* titled "The Power of Helplessness." I sure don't feel any power in my present state of helplessness. Nor do I sense God coming to my aid. All above me, it seems, is a heaven of brass.

My dreams recently have certainly reflected my state:

In one I was the preacher's wife in a church where an elaborate wedding required "tickets" of those invited. I seemed to have arrived late and not really dressed correctly. There was some discussion as to whether I was to be let in without a ticket. Whatever was decided, I never saw the inside of the church in the dream. Instead, because something was missing, a whole group of us had to go and get it—whatever it was. As we went on this errand I kept losing things. First my fur stole, then my gloves. The group grew angry at me; there were even physical threats. I woke with the sense of being odd-man-out, rejected by those who counted.

In another dream I was in an apartment where the plumbing was badly out of order and about to flood the place. I knew where the leak was, but instead of attending to it I left the apartment to go to a meeting where President Nixon was speaking. I was seated in the front row. Since I had left the apartment while sorting the laundry, I still had in my hands a pair of my dad's old dirty work pants and two dirty socks.

During the meeting, I dropped the soiled laundry to the floor and to my chagrin, the President came to where I was sitting, picked up the dirty work pants, looked at them wonderingly, and handed them back to me. Though humiliated, even in my dream came the thought, *But they are soiled not in any shameful way, but through honest work!*

When I got back to the apartment, water covered the floor and the plumber had to be called immediately. Here the dream ended. Clearly, the overflowing water represented some situation that my subconscious knew to be wrong, which I was neglecting to put right.

And still another dream: I was due to make an important speech, but had no time to go back to the hotel and change my clothes. I was told, "No, you'll just have to wear what you have."

This was dreadful because I had on an old skirt and ankle socks. Behind the stage at the auditorium I started to make up my face while several people watched me impatiently. By now I was acutely aware of an auditorium full of people waiting, too.

The makeup was a process of bungling and stumbling. I could not find a lipstick in the various cluttered purses I had with me. Finally I found it and with shaking hands tried to apply the lipstick, while trying to collect my thoughts about what to say in my speech. Thinking about the talk, I absentmindedly applied lipstick around my eyes. Those watching were startled. I tried to wipe off the lipstick, then apply powder on the area. *I'll go in there looking like an old hag,* I thought. There to my great relief the dream ended.

All these dreams have features in common: clutter, disorganization, unpreparedness, unacceptance of me by those around me, unhappiness with myself, a feeling of being threatened by circumstances and the critical attitudes of others.

And in them all—a state of humiliation.

Len . . . I found Catherine sitting in her chair by the bed, listlessly looking through some catalogs. It was 11:30 A.M., a time when ordinarily she would be in her office hard at work on a manuscript. *How do I penetrate the darkness of her spirit?* I asked myself.

"We need to talk," I began.

"What about?"

"You cannot go on like this. We're all deeply concerned about you."

Catherine shrugged. Her eyes went back to her catalogs. My concern for her shifted to irritation. "How can you go against the advice you've so often given to others about wallowing in self-centeredness?"

For a moment her eyes flashed. I welcomed this, preferring anger to apathy. The sparks quickly subsided, however, and she shrugged again. "Just say that I'm wallowing in my sin."

"You are doing exactly that, and what's more, you're enjoying it."

Catherine shifted about uncomfortably. "What do you want me to do?"

"Put the Amy Catherine matter to rest and get on with your life."

The pain inside suddenly shone through. "I can't put it aside."

"Why?"

"I keep seeing her little mouth crying out for help. I can still feel her body in my arms, wanting so much to be held and loved, yearning for health. Every time I try to do any writing these images return to haunt me."

"Why don't we take off for a week? Go down to the Keys, perhaps, or to one of the islands," I suggested.

Catherine brightened for a moment, then shook her head. "I don't think I'd be good company. It's my problem and I'll work through it." She thought for a moment. "What was the title of that *Guideposts* piece by Joe Bishop? 'The Way Out Is the Way Through'? Maybe I should read it again."

"The point of the article is that you don't duck a painful issue, you meet it head-on. Are you doing that?" I asked.

"I'm trying to." She paused for a long moment. "In some ways you know me better than anyone else in the world. In one area you don't know me at all."

"What's that?"

"There's a part of me, deep down, that since my childhood has belonged only to the Person of Jesus Christ. He and I have had some wonderful sharing times together. He has been with me in every crisis—until now." Her lip began to tremble. "Now He just isn't there anymore. Each morning when I awake, I seek Him, to no avail. I must have offended Him terribly this past summer."

I put my arms around her, feeling her pain, fighting back my own tears. "You've been through these dark times before, haven't you? What about those occasions during your widowhood when you felt estranged from God?"

"They were more like dry periods when I was simply unproductive. And they never lasted very long. Sure, I'd be sunk in self-pity for a stretch, but Jesus was somehow close to me even then. For months now there has been real darkness. I feel like I'm talking to the ceiling. And you know how listless my prayers have been."

I nodded. Listless was the right word. "When did you first feel this rejection—if that's what it is?"

For a while Catherine didn't answer. In fact, I had to repeat the question. Her thoughts seemed many miles away.

"I'm not sure," she said at last. "Probably right after Amy Catherine's death. Possibly after hearing about Virginia Lively's prophecy. She heard correctly. I didn't."

"And that hurt your pride."

"She should have told me."

"If she had come up to you in Cape Cod and reported this revelation to you, you would have rejected it flat. I've never seen you so convinced, so determined about anything as you were about Amy Catherine's healing."

"I'll never go out on a limb like that again—for anything or anyone—ever," she snapped.

I took a deep breath. "I think it's your anger at God that has shut the door on your relationship with Him."

She shook her head vigorously. "I've been angry at Him before and He still comforted me. I believe God encourages us to be honest, to express anger when we feel it. So I don't think you're right, Len. Sure I was angry when Amy Catherine died, rebellious, too . . . ." She stopped, hearing her own words.

"There's a big difference between anger and rebellion." I voiced her unspoken thought. "Feelings of anger are often justified, and usually subside fairly quickly. Rebellion is

more long-lasting and destructive. Remember that Bible
class we taught last year? How you kept stressing that it
was the rebellion of the Israelites that kept them from the
Promised Land?"

She nodded. "One's words can come back to haunt one,
can't they?"

"Think about it, Catherine," I urged. "You're miserable
without Jesus. Maybe you should go off somewhere alone
and pray it through."

Catherine . . . Inside I am dry and lonely, unable to accom-
plish anything, really, just going through the motions of
life, barely able to do that. It is more than a dry period. I've
been through those before and did not lose the Presence.
This is darkness. Deadness. Awful in the way it numbs you,
makes you cold and indifferent. You do the very thing, say
the very word, you know you should not. Frightening!

This morning in an effort to find a handhold to pull
myself out of this pit, I reread C.S. Lewis' *Screwtape Letters.* In advising the junior demon, Wormwood, how to turn
Christians away from God, Screwtape warns that at times
their Enemy (God) will withdraw all support from His own
subjects. He continues:

> He cannot "tempt" to virtue as we do to vice. The
> Enemy wants them to learn to walk and must therefore
> take away His hand. . . . Do not be deceived, Worm-
> wood. Our cause is never more in danger than when a
> human, no longer desiring, but still intending, to do
> our Enemy's will, looks round upon a universe from
> which every trace of Him seems to have vanished, and
> asks why he has been forsaken, and still obeys.

I find myself convicted by these words. For I know that
God not only asks us to bear these dry and barren stretches
of life, but even to *thank* Him for them. This is what Glenn

Clark called "radiant acquiescence," a phrase I always
thought was a bit much—and still do, I guess.

I must get down on paper some of the passages I've
encountered this week in my reading of Scripture. Though
my prayers are hollow and uninspired, I *am* receiving instruction from His Word. If the Lord will no longer speak to
me directly, then I will go this route.

Here are the passages I have been led to:

> And when you spread forth your hands in prayer, implor-
> ing help, I will hide My eyes from you; even though you
> make many prayers, I will not hear; your hands are full of
> blood! Wash yourselves; make yourselves clean; put away
> the evil of your doings from before My eyes; cease to do evil.
>
> Isaiah 1:15–16, AMPLIFIED

> The Lord is far from the wicked, but He hears the prayer
> of the [consistently] righteous—the upright, in right stand-
> ing with Him
>
> Proverbs 15:29, AMPLIFIED

> You do ask and yet fail to receive, because you ask with
> wrong purpose and evil, selfish motives. . . . You [are like]
> unfaithful wives [having illicit love affairs with the world]
> and breaking your marriage vow to God!
>
> James 4: 3–4, AMPLIFIED

These verses are like arrows piercing my heart. Lord,
have mercy.

During my afternoon nap I had yet another version of a
dream that has recurred over and over again. I am always in
a very large house. I go through corridors and rooms, from
one floor to another. There are many people around, but
they pay no attention to me, and I have nothing to do with
them, do not appear to know them. I am searching, search-

ing for my own room, my own place, but cannot find it. I
cannot even find which floor it's on. Fear is in the dream,
building to panic. Sometimes, in exhaustion, I even stop in
someone else's room to take a nap in order to get strength to
rise and start searching again.

Usually I awaken from this recurring dream with my
stomach hurting and symptoms of severe tension, probably
with raised blood pressure.

"In My Father's house are many mansions. . . ." This passage used to comfort me because it promises a place for
everyone. I do have a place in the universe. Why am I now
so lost?

This terrible feeling of lostness—apparently deep in my
subconscious—must reflect my separation from God.
When one has lost one's way and can no longer feel the
Shepherd's hand, when the Valley of the Shadow is dark
with the light of faith withdrawn, what does one do then?

Trust God in the dark and wait and hope and hang on as
best one can, I suppose.

Len . . . Christmas in our home had always been a lively
family time, I had hoped that Christmas 1971 would lift
Catherine out of her darkness. It did not.

I'd expected her to be impressed with the changes in
Linda when she came home for the holidays. Linda seemed
more disciplined, was handling her finances well, and
hadn't asked us for a penny. Gone was the confusion of
the '60s as she launched into her new job in full-time
Christian work with college students. But though Catherine complimented Linda on these things, the compli-
ments seemed dutiful rather than heartfelt.

Chester was enjoying his second year at Taylor University in Upland, Indiana, a rising star on the Taylor tennis
team. Ordinarily Catherine would have drawn him out
about the semester's experiences; this Christmas—beyond
a few perfunctory inquiries—she showed little curiosity.

Jeffrey, attending a local prep school, had found work for the holidays in a nearby restaurant. As he regaled us with tales of difficult customers and crises in the kitchen, Catherine seemed miles away, her mind wandering down a dark road where none of us could follow.

Peter, Edith, and Mary Elizabeth had not been able to come to Florida this Christmas because of Peter's heavy responsibilities to his congregation at the holiday season. Amy Catherine's brief life and death had left unresolved questions with which both families were still struggling.

Catherine . . . I have received some illumination about this shut-in place in which I have been so confined. It came from a section in *Mysticism*, by Evelyn Underhill, entitled "Dark Night of the Soul."

She explains that for those who have trod the Christian way for some time, a spiritual and psychic fatigue can creep in. In this state one knows anew the helplessness of the human condition. In fact, here, for a time, we can be in a worse state than at the beginning of our Christian walk. The reason: when one first becomes a Christian, along with new awareness of one's own frailty, there is the sure and wonderful knowledge of God's *adequacy*. In the darkness that assails the long-time Christian, the skies seem totally deaf; no light breaks through at all. Nothing, inside and outside, seems to work.

This is certainly my state at this time.

According to Evelyn Underhill, if one can ride it through on sheer, blind faith, just hanging onto the rock of salvation, then it has to pass, and we go on to a higher state in the spiritual life.

What was a fresh thought to me was that this dark state is *necessary* in our Christian growth. It comes when we've reached a kind of plateau of faith where nothing is changing, where certain areas of our life remain *not* committed to Jesus Christ, *not* being taken over by Him. So we have to find fresh truths in our helplessness and in our need, become desperate in a new way, in order to get on with the next stage in our Christian development.

Even many great Christian saints went through a "dark night" experience, some pretty gruesome, according to Underhill, before they came out into the light again. This is encouraging for us ordinary strugglers!

More on "The Dark Night" from Evelyn Underhill: "The most intense period of that great swing-back into darkness . . . is seldom lit by visions or made homely by voices. . . . Stagnation . . . impotence, blankness, solitude, are the epithets by which those immersed in this *dark fire of purification* describe their pains."

I paused a moment to reflect. Was I being purified? I saw none of that, at least not yet. There was stagnation, all right, more like sloth.

"Psychologically considered," Underhill wrote, "the Dark Night is an example of the operation of the law of reaction from stress. It is a period of fatigue and lassitude following a period of sustained mystical activity."

Again I paused to consider. Yes, stress had built up to an incredible high during the six weeks of Amy Catherine's life. Then the awful letdown, followed by total fatigue. But I've been through these highs and lows before and never lost contact with Jesus.

When one's mental machinery has been overworked, continued Underhill, "when the higher centres [of the mind] have been submitted to the continuous strain . . . with its accompanying periods of intense fervour . . . the swing-back into the negative state occurs almost of necessity.

"This is the psychological explanation of those strange and painful episodes in the lives of great saints—indeed, of many spiritual persons hardly to be classed as saints—when, perhaps after a long life . . . with growing consciousness of the 'presence of God,' the whole inner experience is suddenly swept away, and only a blind reliance on past convictions saves them from unbelief. The great contemplatives . . . emerge from this period of destitution, however long and drastic it may be, as from a new purification. It is for them the gateway to a higher state. But persons of a less heroic spirituality, if they enter the Night at all, may succumb to its dangers and pains. This 'great negation' is the sorting-house of the spiritual life."

Many succumb to its pains. That certainly describes my unheroic reaction to the current darkness. Yet it is reassuring to know that those who hungered most for God were often the ones deprived for the longest stretches. I want to learn more about the saints. . . .

Evelyn Underhill went on to describe the "dark night" experience of Madame Guyon (1648–1717). Looking further into her life I found that this fascinating woman was a member of high French society and the mother of five children. Jeanne Guyon above all else was an all-out woman of God. She was imprisoned in the Bastille for four years because of her religious beliefs, which were at odds with the Roman Catholic Church of that period. She wrote forty books, including a twenty-volume commentary on the Bible. Though one of the leading exponents of *Quietism*— which teaches that spiritual perfection is attained in an attitude of total acquiescence to circumstances in life— Madame Guyon was noted for her Christian philanthropy: dispensing bread to the poor, taking the sick into her home, establishing hospitals in several cities.

Yet Madame Guyon experienced painful periods of what she called "aridity" (what writer hasn't gone through that?), during which she lost for a time all interest in "the divine realities" that had previously filled her life. "How dearly I paid for those happy periods when the presence of God was so real," Madame Guyon wrote in her autobiography. "For this possession which seemed to me so perfect was but the preparation for times of total deprivation."

During these dark times intellectual life sank to a low ebb. She suffered trials of every kind: "exterior and interior crosses abounded."

When her consciousness of God was extinguished, a state of mental and moral chaos seems to have invaded Madame Guyon. "As soon as I perceived happiness or beauty or a virtue," she stated, "it seemed to me that I fell incessantly into the contrary vice: [for example] if I was given an intense perception of the purity of God, so far as my feelings went, I myself became more and more impure. My imagination was in a state of appalling confusion. . . . I could not perceive any good thing that I had done in my whole life."

Self-control and the power of attention were diminished. She became attracted to the worldly things around her, which she had previously renounced. The neat edifice of her spiritual life was in ruins.

"It is an amazing thing," said Madame Guyon, "for a soul that believed herself to be advanced in the way of perfection, when she sees herself thus go to pieces all at once." Although she watched her husband and their two eldest children die early on, faced the hardships of travel as a missionary of the Gospel, relinquished her life as a wealthy socialite to minister to the poorest of the poor during the days of Louis XIV, then for years suffered the "dark night" when she felt that even God had abandoned her, Madame Guyon was restored to health in her final years to teach the word. "He did return with more goodness and strength and with great splendor." In her last will and testament, Madame Guyon wrote:

It is to Thee, O Lord God, that I owe all things; and it is to Thee, that I now surrender up all that I am. Do with me, O my God, whatsoever Thou pleasest. . . .

Within Thy hands, O God, I leave my soul, not relying
for my salvation on any good that is in me, but solely
on Thy mercies, and the merits and sufferings of my
Lord Jesus Christ.

I've never approached either Madame Guyon's total dedi-
cation or the total breakdown she went through; the
thought that the road back to communion with God leads
through such suffering terrifies me.

In the Valley —————————

*L*en ... As the months went by, those of us in daily contact with Catherine—her mother, our secretary Jeanne Sevigny, our housekeeper, Mary Moncur, our son Jeffrey, and I—were baffled and distressed by Catherine's state. To outsiders she appeared to be living a normal life; to the five of us (Chet was back at school, Linda at work in Washington, D.C.) she was but a shell of the woman we knew and loved.

Catherine and I arose early as always, having a time of Bible reading and prayer together before beginning our work day. But the prayer time was wooden; Catherine was mouthing words by rote. There was no vitality, no joy, no power. Whether I was tender or scolding, patient or angry made no difference. She responded lethargically.

After breakfast she went to her office to write. "How is she doing?" I would ask Jeanne Sevigny. Jeanne, by now a close friend and a participant in our ministry as well as secretary, would just shake her head. "Productivity about zero."

"Nothing at all?"

"Nothing for me to type. She keeps reading over parts of the *Gloria* manuscript, but we all know that project is dead. A part of her seemed to die with it. We do get the mail answered, but I have to push and shove and prod her even with that."

"What's your diagnosis, Jeanne?"

"Grief and frustration. Anger, too."

"Aimed at whom?"

"God, mostly. And at us, too. All of us, even her mother."

"Buried anger, isn't it? She doesn't explode as she used to."

"You're right. I think the explosions were a lot healthier."

My efforts toward dialogue with Catherine were mostly unsuccessful. After receiving a series of one-word answers to my questions, I would usually back off. Yet I knew I had to keep trying. If only something would go right for her! The movie version of her novel *Christy* seemed permanently shelved; likewise her novel *Gloria*, though she kept pulling the manuscript from the file drawer and going through the motions of working on it. Amy Catherine had died. The relationship with Peter and Edith was strained. In fact, none of her relationships was working very well.

The best news I had to give her was about Linda, who continued to astonish me with the changes in her life. "Linda has found a most remarkable group of Christian friends," I told Catherine one day in our bedroom after I had visited Linda in Washington at the nonprofit organization "Cornerstone" where she worked. "In addition to her administrative responsibilities and leading a Bible study, Linda writes a newsletter. I think she has a gift for writing."

No response.

"Tell me something, Catherine. Why do you refuse to see the many positive results of Amy Catherine's short life? She was used in a mighty way, you know."

Catherine looked at me wearily. "I'm glad for Linda, and for Scott Ross and Pam Gordon and Jamie Buckingham and all the others who were helped. It's very self-centered of me not to be more grateful for this, I know. Forgive me."

"You say that, but you don't mean it. Words are coming out of you, but there's no emotion to back them up. It's as if the real you has gone somewhere else and I'm talking to a cardboard figure."

"Thank you for those kind words."

I shifted to a different line. "You said several days ago that you felt you were moving about in a dark cage. Do you mean something like a prison?"

"That's pretty close."

"What are you doing to get out?"

"Not enough, I guess. I feel like a dead person. Abandoned."

"Not by those of us here in this house. We love you. We're praying for you."

"Thank you."

I sat down on the bed where she was sitting and reached for her hand. "I've heard you say many times that when a lot of things go wrong in a person's life, the Lord is trying to get that person's attention. I'm sure you've been applying this to yourself."

For the first time, Catherine's eyes met mine. "I sure have."

"What do you think He's saying to you?"

Long pause. "That I'm probably out of His will. That I may have been out of His will for some time."

There was sudden tension between us; a warning light within me cautioned me to cease the probing. Yet another part of me knew I must push ahead.

"How long do you think you've been out of His will?"

The question lay there between us for a moment. Both of us knew where we were heading. Catherine's eyes left mine and her lip trembled.

"Since I married you," she finally said.

"You know and I know that everything hasn't gone wrong since we were married," I challenged her. "Forget all the books and articles we've worked on together and their impact on people. Look at the lives of our four children. Has our marriage made things better for them or worse?"

"Better, I guess. But I think you could have married any number of women who would have been better mothers to your children. I just think that I was supposed to stay single after Peter's death."

"And live all alone in that comfortable sanctuary you were building . . . a snug retreat . . . well away from the action. That's not the guidance you got before we were married. After warning you that it would be difficult at times, the Lord nudged you to say yes to a new life with me."

Catherine nodded. "I remember. But I'm not at all sure about my guidance anymore. I thought I heard the Lord say He was going to heal Amy Catherine. Obviously I heard Him wrong. Maybe I heard Him wrong about us."

I sat there a moment struggling with a decision. How to reach Catherine? Gentleness and patience? Or confrontation? I made up my mind.

"Would you like to hear my opinion as to when you began to move away from God's will?"

Catherine stared at me stonily. "Go ahead."

"It all began with the enormous success of Christy. I watched the change in you. It was gradual over many months. The plaudits, the adulation, the bestseller lists, the movie sale, all heady stuff. When we flew to New York for interviews, the publisher insisted on providing a limousine. We both loved it. Then came the bowing and scraping by the editors when you described your next book, another novel.

What they were saying, essentially, Catherine, was that you could do no wrong. That's when the change in you really began. Deep down inside, you bought it. You began to think you could do no wrong. Every book you'd written, a major success. Magazines eager for articles."

I paused, watching Catherine's reaction. She didn't appear resistant so I plunged ahead.

"It was at this point, Catherine, that I began to feel the arrogance. Before the success of *Christy* you had what I felt was a delightful sense of inadequacy. Especially for one who had been so successful. It was this inadequacy that I related to when we first met. You needed God. Without Him you were incomplete. In a lesser way you needed me. We made a good team in both work and play. On your book projects you needed Tib. Then after *Christy* you changed. Ask yourself, Catherine. Did you come to a point where you felt you didn't need God anymore? Or me? Or anyone?"

Catherine flared. "I've always needed God."

"If you've always needed Him, why can't you reach Him now?"

A stricken look clouded Catherine's face. Tears welled up. I tried to embrace her, but she turned away. I patted her shoulder for a few minutes, then left her alone.

Catherine . . . I am forced to the conclusion that Len is right. I did become spiritually arrogant after *Christy*. I became selfish with the use of my time, not wanting to be bothered with people who bored me or disagreed with me. I forgot too easily what I owed to the skills of others.

God was right to discipline me. I deserved it. Len was right to correct me.

But did the punishment fit the crime? I now feel so completely abandoned, rejected. The pain of Amy Catherine's death still immobilizes me. It's so dreadful to be in a state of darkness that I can understand better the fear of hell. How awful eternal darkness must be!

Reading about the "dark night" in Evelyn Underhill's *Mysticism* both helps me and depresses me. Her description of the pain and anguish suffered by St. Teresa of Avila, the sixteenth-century Spanish Carmelite, is agonizingly real to me.

Is there something inside those great saints that invites, even seeks this kind of suffering? The holy men and women of medieval times actually even inflicted torture upon themselves as a way to subdue their flesh and thus come to know God better. I confess I'm baffled by this. Life is painful enough without making it more so. Some of these godly people make it sound as if the dark night experience should be deeply relished because it will end up being good for you.

Reading further in Evelyn Underhill's book, I see that St. Catherine of Siena was another who went through intense suffering and spiritual warfare. She came out of a well-to-do Italian family and as a girl was described as "pert, pretty and pious." Early on, she determined to remain a virgin, with Jesus only as her Bridegroom. Despite strong parental resistance she entered a convent.

After enjoying the presence of Christ for many years, however, there came a dark night experience. For months on end Catherine was tormented by fiends who filled her small cell in the convent "with obscene words and gestures inviting her to lust."

Try as she would, she obtained no relief from this assault until she ceased her opposition. Her surrender consisted of this simple statement: "I . . . will gladly bear these and all other torments in the name of the Saviour, for as long as it shall please His Majesty." With this act, the evil spirits fled and she was comforted by a vision of the cross.

St. Teresa had a similar experience that she attributed to the action of the devil. "The soul," she says, ". . . loses all control over itself, and all power of thinking of anything but the absurdities he puts before it. . . . It is impossible to describe the sufferings of the soul in this state. It goes about in quest of relief, and God suffers it to find none."

St. Teresa then goes on to describe the inner pain there is in separation from God: "The pain thus grows to such a degree that in spite of herself the sufferer gives vent to loud cries, which she cannot stifle, however patient and accustomed to pain she may be, because this is not a pain which is felt in the body, but in the depths of the soul. . . . You will . . . ask why this soul does not conform herself to His will. . . . Hitherto she could do this, and consecrated her life to it; but now she cannot, for her reason is reduced to such a state that she is no longer mistress of herself and can think of nothing but her affliction."

I'm not ready to identify with Teresa's former consecration and total self-surrender, but I can relate to the loneliness she felt, her self-centeredness, her inability to take the positive action, to do what would get her going in the right direction. Until one has been immobilized, one does not understand this kind of paralysis. I feel like a person suspended in midair, who can neither touch the earth nor mount to heaven.

Evelyn Underhill points out that all these forms of the dark night—the absence of God, the sense of sin, the loss of the self's old peace and joy, and its apparent relapse to lower spiritual and mental levels—are considered by the mystics themselves to be a purification of the will so that it may be merged with God's will.

The starved and tortured spirit going through a dark night, Underhill writes, learns "to accept lovelessness for the sake of Love, nothingness for the sake of the all, [to die] without any sure promise of life. It sees with amazement the most sure foundations of its transcendental life crumble beneath it, dwells in a darkness which seems to hold no promise of a dawn."

Then in her *Dialogue* St. Catherine records these words, which she felt God spoke to her:

"In order to raise the soul from imperfection," says the Voice of God, "I withdraw Myself from her sentiment, depriving her of former consolations . . . which I do in order to humiliate her, and cause her to seek Me in truth. . . . Then, if she loved Me without thought of self . . . she rejoices in the time of trouble, deeming herself unworthy of peace and quietness of mind. . . . Though she perceives that I have withdrawn Myself . . . [she] perseveres with humility in her exercises . . . and it is to this end . . . that I withdraw from her. . . . I leave her so that she may see and know her defects . . . and learn how incapable she is of stability or perseverance. . . . This should be the end and purpose of all her self-knowledge, to rise above herself. . . ."

There is much in this statement to ponder. My mind accepts the idea that God may be doing a purification of my soul by withdrawing Himself. Humiliation is something I am now very familiar with. I have always seen God as a tender, loving Father. That He can also be rigorous and stern is now abundantly clear to me as well.

In reading about these Christian saints and mystics, I'm reminded that though the way we talk about our faith changes, the basic truths of Christianity do not. *Ego-slaying* is a modern term for the process St. Catherine went through. It was a concept I thought I'd come to grips with in *Beyond Our Selves*. I'm forced to the conclusion now that though I may have assented intellectually to this principle, I have done little to live it out.

There are other popular phrases to describe it. "The Cross life" is the one used today in many Christian groups; "self-abandonment" is another. Whatever the words used, the underlying reality is the same: *For there to be more of God in a person's life, there has to be less of self.*

No one demonstrated that principle better than the Ger-

man saint Heinrich Suso. Evelyn Underhill was greatly
intrigued by Suso and I can understand why.

Len . . . Catherine's interest in Heinrich Suso's dark night
experience led me to do some research of my own on this
German saint. It's a story that would have made front page
news if it had happened today.

Suso was born about 1300 in the German province of
Swabia, the son of a knight and a patrician mother. His
early life was lived on the banks of Lake Constance, with
the towering Alps in the background.

By nature young Heinrich was a poet. Even his prose was
full of the song of the birds and the scent of flowers. His
father is described as "a very worldly man" whose life
centered on hunting, hawking, and tournaments. Heinrich,
however, took after his religious and tenderhearted mother.

His frail health preventing his becoming a knight,
Heinrich entered the Dominican friary of Constance at thirteen. At eighteen, hungering for more of God, he entered
into strict seclusion which was to last for nine years. He
practiced severe bodily mortifications: he wore a hairshirt
and an iron collar around his neck to which his hands were
fastened. A wooden cross with iron nails in it was attached
to his back. When his health had been broken by these
excesses, one day in a vision the Lord told him to desist.
The very next day he threw all his torture instruments into
the river.

Suso went to Cologne to complete his studies, then returned to Constance to teach there in the friary house. This
was difficult for him at first because he loved to be alone in
rapt communion with God. At once artist and recluse,
utterly impractical, he had the dreamer's dread of the world
of men.

Suso was a born romantic. Images of a spiritual chivalry
color his devotional writings: again and again he turns to
the language of the tournament. Suso was exalted by the

stories of hard combats, the knightly fortitude that pays no attention to its wounds.

"O my sweet Lord," he exclaimed one day, "if only I could become Thy spiritual knight!" When he experienced trials, however, Suso went off by himself to sulk. In his writings he reported the Lord's response: "Well, now, Heinrich, what has become of your noble chivalry? Who is this knight of straw? It is not by making rash promises and drawing back when suffering comes that the victory is won."

"Alas! Lord," said Suso plaintively, "the tournaments in which one must suffer for Thee last such a very long time!"

The Lord replied, "But the reward and the honor which I give to My knights endure forever."

God was calling Suso to give more of himself to others, to have more contact with the unfriendly world. Instead of the quiet cell and the secret mortifications, the reality of his renunciation was to be tested under the unsympathetic gaze of other men. For the outside world was to test Suso to his utmost.

It happened during one of his teaching tours. A woman who attended one of his services accused him of being the father of her child. This kind of news always spreads like a forest fire on a windy day. Poor Suso was utterly crushed by the ensuing uproar, "wounded to the depths of his heart."

"Lord, Lord!" he cried. "Every day of my life I have worshiped Thy holy name, and have helped to cause it to be loved and honored by many men: I am blameless in this situation and now Thou wouldst drag my name through the mud!"

The Lord did not answer.

When the scandal was at its height, a woman close to the pregnant woman came to Suso in secret. To his speechless horror she offered to destroy the child that was the cause of this gossip, in order that the tale might be quickly forgotten. "Unless the baby is somehow disposed of," she warned, "you will be forced by public opinion to accept it and provide for its upbringing."

How would an intrepid knight handle such a dilemma? Suso wondered. To the woman he said, "Your plan is unthinkable. I have confidence in the God of heaven, who is rich, and who has given me until now all that which was needful unto me. He will help me to keep, if need be, another beside myself. Please go and fetch the little child that I may see it."

When the woman returned with the baby boy, Suso put him on his knees. Sighing deeply, Suso said, "Could I kill a pretty baby that smiled at me? No, no, I had rather suffer every trial that could come upon me!

"Oh, my poor, poor child," he continued. "Thou art an unfortunate orphan, for thy unnatural father hath denied thee and thy wicked mother would cast thee off. The providence of God hath given thee to me, in order that I may provide thy upkeep. I will accept thee, then, from Him and from no one else."

How different a response would have come from the early Suso, an aesthetic man interested in little but his own safe spirituality, a man who would have rejected the child self-righteously as someone else's problem.

Heinrich Suso found a suitable woman to care for the child at his expense. When the news of his decision to support the baby circulated through the community, his reputation was further damaged. Now even his friends forsook him and he narrowly escaped expulsion from his religious order. For by assuming the expense of rearing the child, Suso seemed to admit that he was, in effect, the real father—though he was not.

This all-out act of chivalry should have won for Suso the approval of heaven, if not of men. But if heaven applauded, Heinrich Suso could not hear it. He entered a darkness where even God seemed to have turned His back. In despair, he implored his Lord, "Why have You allowed this to happen to me?"

There was only silence. Suso traveled to Ulm where he tried to begin a new ministry. But the story of "his child" followed him and he was forced to flee again.

From Suso's biography it appears that his "dark night of the soul" lasted a full ten years. He remained a friar, he continued to write and teach, but he was bitter and rebellious and not very productive. At some point near the end of this dark period there came a dialogue with God. It began with Suso asking the question, "Where are You in my travail, Lord?"

After years of silence, he at last heard God's voice: *Heinrich, where then is your resignation? Where is that equal humor in joy and in tribulation which you have taught other men to love?*

Suso replied, weeping, "You ask where is my resignation? But tell me first, where is the infinite mercy of God for His friends? Thou knowest that Thou art my only consolation, that all my trust is only in Thee. So long as it was only a question of preaching resignation, that was easy: but now that my heart is pierced, now that I am wounded to the marrow . . . how can I be resigned?"

Then, abandoning himself completely, he concluded, "If it cannot be otherwise, *fiat voluntas tua* (be it done according to Your will)."

This act of self-abandonment was at once followed by a vision from the Lord in which the end of his troubles was announced.

Suso summed up his experience thus: "When God judged that it was time, He rewarded me for all my suffering. I then enjoyed peace of heart and received in tranquillity and quietness many precious graces. I came to praise the Lord from the very depths of my soul for those same sufferings which, for all the world, I would not now have been spared. And God caused me to understand that by this complete abasement I had gained more, and was made the more worthy to be raised up to God, than by all the pains which I had suffered from my youth up to that time."

Catherine . . . The suffering saints—and I should include Job here, too—make my troubles seem small and paltry indeed, but their ordeals continue to frighten me. Is this the kind of cross life the Lord wants all of us to live?

If so, why does the Bible promise in so many places "good things" for those who love the Lord?

Did Suso and the others have a certain kind of spiritual pride that the Lord found obnoxious and that needed to be demolished?

More to the point, do I have this same kind of spiritual pride and is my dark night experience His way of chastening me?

I find myself with many questions and few answers.

I have never had a problem facing up to the fact that I am a sinner. Since the fall of Eve in the Garden of Eden human nature has been sinful. Glibly I can repeat, "I am a sinner saved by grace."

By saying this, however, I place myself in a general category of sinners, enabling me to avoid facing up to the fact that I have committed, am committing, specific sins. It is much more comfortable to be general than specific. The other day I ran up against this phrase in *My Utmost for His Highest* by Oswald Chambers: "Sin is red-handed mutiny against God."

That hit me like a sledgehammer blow. I am in rebellion against God. I have been for many months now. I am in despair about it, but cannot seem to change. All is darkness in my life. Nothing is working. I read books, I go to church, Len and I pray together, but Jesus is not in any of it.

My sin is separating me from God—Father, Son, and Holy Spirit. Chambers also says, "If sin rules in me, God's life in me will be killed; if God rules in me, sin in me will be killed."

How do I make that switch so that again God rules in me?

I do not want to go through a ten-year period of darkness as Heinrich Suso did.

A Shaft
of Light _____

*L*en . . . One morning in the spring of 1972 two of Catherine's closest women friends—Virginia Lively, Freddie Koch—and I asked Catherine to join us in the living room of our Boynton Beach home. We were all struck by her joylessness, her heavy spirit, and by the deep circles under her eyes. Sleeplessness was becoming more and more of a major problem for her.

We talked aimlessly for a few moments, then Catherine, always blunt, cut it short. "You're here to confront me," she stated. "Let's get on with it."

"We've tried to be helpful to you several times since Amy

Catherine's death," Freddie began. "You admit you're in trouble, we pray together, and nothing happens. Why?"

Catherine shrugged, then waved her hand in a helpless gesture. "I wish I knew."

"Are you still angry at God?" asked Virginia.

Catherine hesitated a moment. "Who am I to be angry at God? He is our almighty Lord, who knows all, sees all, and has His own ways that are mysterious and incomprehensible to us. It would be awfully silly for me to pit my puny anger against the Almighty."

"Yet that's what you've been doing for the past six months," I stated.

For a moment I hoped Catherine was going to deny it, argue back with her old zest. But she quickly subsided into passivity.

"What's happened in the past six months isn't as important as what happens in the future," Virginia enjoined. "We love you, Catherine, and it hurts us all to see you suffering."

Freddie Koch drew a deep breath and said, "Catherine, I feel the Lord is telling me something that He wants me to tell you. It's about your self-pity. You're neck-deep in self-pity."

Catherine nodded unemotionally. "I think that's probably right. I confess to being a mess. So how do I get out of this hole? I'm sick to death of the darkness in my life."

"You could really be sick to death unless you do something about it, Catherine," said Virginia.

"The first step is to confess the rebellion and self-pity to the Lord," I suggested softly. "Confession and repentance."

Catherine shrugged hopelessly. "I've already done this, again and again. I honestly have. It's the complete lack of response that confounds me. I've never, ever lived in this kind of vacuum before. I talk, I pray. Nothing. For most of my life I've felt God's presence, heard His voice, received thoughts that I knew came from Him. No more. He's gone from my life. I know I terribly offended Him last August. I guess I offended most everybody. But I was so totally caught up in the Amy Catherine battle. It was all-out warfare, you know. Nothing ever like it." Tears began spilling out of her eyes.

"What is destroying me is that I understand nothing about it, nothing about anything that happened. What's wrong with going all-out for something you believe in? God likes single-eyed people, doesn't He? It says so in Scripture. Well, I've always tried to be one hundred percent in everything I do. And always before, God honored my efforts. Why not this time? Why have I been flattened so completely? I know it's happened to others. Great saints have gone through dark nights a thousand times worse than mine. But they almost seemed to ask for it, seeking some higher plane of spirituality. I didn't ask for anything for myself, only that a tiny baby be healed, and God not only refused that request, but turned His back on me. I don't understand."

"Maybe it's that insistence on understanding that's the problem, Catherine," suggested Virginia.

Catherine stared at Virginia for a moment with a hint of surprise in her eyes.

Something stirred in me. Had we made a small breakthrough in Catherine's impenetrable shell?

When the session broke up after a prayer time, I was still not sure.

Catherine . . . Something happened to me yesterday when Virginia, Freddie, Len, and I met. For a moment a shaft of light seemed to break through the darkness. When I awoke this morning, however, the darkness still surrounded me. My prayers still seemed to bounce back from the ceiling.

Then for the first time in months a new and gentle thought came to rest on my mind: *Read Isaiah 53.* It didn't come from my thoughts, nor would Satan likely be sending me to Scripture. With a surge of hope, I knew it had to be from the Lord.

I read the 53rd chapter of Isaiah eagerly, struck anew by this foretelling of how Jesus would suffer hatred and rejection, of how alone He would be on the cross. These passages leapt out at me:

> He was oppressed and he was afflicted, yet he never said a word. . . . He was buried like a criminal . . . but he had done no wrong. . . . Yet it was the Lord's good plan to bruise him and fill him with grief.
>
> Isaiah 53:7,9–10, TLB

I had read this passage many times before, even since Amy Catherine's death, but it had not affected me as it did now, particularly the tenth verse. God made His own Son suffer, but it was a "good plan." More than "good," it was perfect as only something from God could be. It was terribly important to the future of the human race that Jesus Christ have His dark night experience on the cross. Yet what a desperately dark night it had to be for Him, a time of despair and abandonment for Him to have cried out, "My God, my God, why hast thou forsaken me?" (Matthew 27:46).

Suddenly I was overwhelmed with feelings of remorse, embarrassment, gratitude, and relief, all mingled together. Reading about the saints and their trials had not touched or enlightened me the way this sudden realization had. For reasons of His own, God had allowed Amy Catherine to be born genetically damaged. Her death served God's purposes, fulfilled His plan in some specific way not revealed to us, just as Christ's death on the cross at first baffled and dismayed His disciples, but did not destroy their faith. I heard my own words, "What is destroying me is that I don't understand." I, from my tiny human vantage point, demanding to see into the secrets of eternity!

Virginia had challenged me on it: "Maybe it's that insistence on understanding that's the problem, Catherine."

How many others had tried to caution me? Linda, reading from Isaiah: "Maybe we aren't supposed to understand why God does certain things."

Tib, with one of the best minds I know: "Just because I don't understand something doesn't mean it isn't so."

What about the weeks after Peter Marshall's death when my plea for understanding had been met with something infinitely greater?

Instead of feeling rejected and abandoned, I suddenly felt ashamed. When Amy Catherine died, I demanded that God explain Himself to me, and when He didn't, I proceeded to sulk like a child. A petulant child who had failed to get her own way.

In the days that followed this new understanding, I began to pore over the Scripture accounts of Jesus' humiliation and death; also Bible commentaries on this theme. I was especially moved by this passage from a book by Hans Kung, *On Being a Christian*, portraying how the death of Jesus might have looked to a news reporter the day after the crucifixion:

Jesus found himself left alone, not only by his people, but by the One to whom he had constantly appealed as no one did before him. Left absolutely alone. We do not know what Jesus thought and felt as he was dying. But it is obvious to the whole world that he had proclaimed the early advent of God in his kingdom and this God did not come. A God who was man's friend, knowing all his needs, close to him, but this God was absent.

The unique communion with God which he had seemed to enjoy only makes his forsakenness more unique. This God and Father with whom he had iden-

tified himself to the very end did not at the end identify himself with the sufferer. And so everything
seemed as if it had never been: in vain. He who had
announced the closeness and advent of God his Father
publicly before the whole world died utterly forsaken
by God and was thus publicly demonstrated as godless
before the whole world: someone judged by God himself, disposed of once and for all.

What better description of estrangement from God—*yet
this was His dearly beloved Son!*

If Jesus could suffer this humiliation before the whole
world, what right did I have to sulk and pout because I had
been made to look foolish before a few friends and fellow
Christians?

Day after day in our Florida home, I shut myself away
with my Bible and notebook to work through my new
discoveries, seeking a new relationship with my Lord.

Again and again I read the crucifixion account, feeling
the aloneness, the agony, the abandonment Jesus must have
felt. I was there in the crowd, looking up into His face.

Flooded anew by contrition one afternoon, I burst into
tears and stumbled to my knees. "Forgive me, Lord. Forgive
me for my rejection of You, too."

Then came this revelation: when life hands us situations
we cannot understand, we have one of two choices. We can
wallow in misery, separated from God. Or we can tell Him,
"I need You and Your presence in my life more than I need
understanding. I choose You, Lord. I trust You to give me
understanding and an answer to all my 'Why's?'—*only if
and when* You choose."

Understanding. That seemed to be the key word in my
difficulties. I had sought it from the Lord most of my life
and in His gentle tenderness He had often provided it. So

often, in fact, that I had begun to take it for granted, assumed I had a right to understanding. What arrogance! What presumption!

Then a new thought hit me like a thunderbolt. *Presumption* was my sin. During the prayers for Amy Catherine I had taken the lead in *telling* God what He was to do about Amy Catherine: "Thank You, Lord, for healing this tiny, precious baby." Had I really heard Him say what *His* plan was for her? Or had I wanted the healing so badly I simply imagined He must, too? *Presumption*. I had assumed something I had no right to assume. God would always be God. We will never fathom His ways, but I had presumed to try. "O Lord, forgive me for my presumption."

Then still another thought struck me. Worse than my presumption, even, was the fact that with Amy Catherine I had really wanted to play God, to be God in her life. Appalled, I tried to detach myself from this sin. There was no detachment. I had tried to usurp the power of almighty God. "O Lord, can You forgive me for this abomination?"

And He answered me. At long, long last, I heard the Voice that had been silent for so many months: *I, your God, am in everything. The baby died, but Amy Catherine is with Me. And while she lived, she ministered to everyone who prayed for her. You alone, Catherine, were too stubborn to see it.*

Section IV
The Coming
of the Light

A Journey Begun _____

*L*en ... During the months that Catherine walked the valley of apathy, I had looked at every hopeful sign as a possible turning point. It came with her words of submission: *I want You, Lord, more than I want understanding.*

I thought back to a time when my own insistence upon "understanding" from God had gotten me into trouble. "Why haven't you healed Eve of alcoholism since we both had committed our lives to You?" I had pleaded. We never seem to learn that God's ways are almost always different from ours.

Now that the turning point had come for Catherine, I sensed that the way from darkness to light would not be easy; her spiritual well was dry. Fortunately for this book, Catherine wrote daily in her journal. °

Catherine . . . The message to me yesterday was most specific. I am to arise each morning at 6 A.M. and rejoice in the Lord. I am to praise Him with a grateful heart. I am to pour out my love for Him. I am to thank Him for everything that has gone wrong in my life. I am to do this indefinitely.

Resistance wells up inside me. I have trouble enough sleeping at nights without rising an hour earlier. But so be it. Len agreed to join me.

So this morning we sit on our patio watching the sunrise. First there was total darkness, then a deep rose above the blue. Now the edges of clouds are showing lighter rose. The birds have awakened and started twittering.

To put the focus on praise, I turned to Psalm 66:

> Make a joyful noise unto God, all ye lands: Sing forth the honour of his name: make his praise glorious.
>
> verses 1–2

Lord, my praise seems so hollow and shallow.

Then I came to verse 18: "If I regard iniquity in my heart, the Lord will not hear me." That is a jolting thought! I have spent so much time in recent months taking my spiritual temperature, bemoaning my sins and faults. The implication of this verse is clear: I am to take my eyes off myself and fix them on Him.

Again this morning I am so aware of my spiritual emptiness. In the days ahead I am to fill myself with spiritual refreshment through beautiful writings the Lord will bring to my mind. I am to let my soul bask in these words until it is aglow. I am to write them down. I am to keep doing it even though my heart is not in it.

Right away these words come to mind:

> *Still, still with Thee,*
> *when purple morning breaketh,*

> *When the bird waketh,*
> *and the shadows flee;*
> *Fairer than morning,*
> *lovelier than daylight,*
> *Dawns the sweet consciousness*
> *I am with Thee.*

Harriet Beecher Stowe, 1811–1896

I feel a flutter in my spirit, Lord. These lines were given me. I could never have recalled them word for word on my own.

This morning, Lord, I am reminded of the pastor and his wife who visited us that New Year's Day (after the "Chair Episode" with Jeff the night before). I remember the story the pastor told of the man who lost his young daughter through an illness. Only by praising God was he healed of his bitterness. This is happening to me now, Lord. I am feeling Your presence again after so many months of darkness. Today I am led to the 90th psalm and these words:

> O satisfy us early with thy mercy; that we may rejoice and be glad all our days.
> Make us glad according to the days wherein thou hast afflicted us, and the years wherein we have seen evil.
> Let thy work appear unto thy servants, and thy glory unto their children.
> And let the beauty of the Lord our God be upon us. . . .
> verses 14–17, KJV

The word *mercy* reverberates within me. You are a merciful God. You saw my rebellion, my arrogance, and chastened me by withdrawing Your presence for a time, but You did not abandon me. Thank You, Lord, for being so loving and patient with me.

The Lord is showing me this morning that my rebellion against Him following Amy Catherine's death was the central element in my sin. Rebellion was the pivotal point on which all the other unlovely qualities turned:

Presumption
Hardness of heart
Self-centeredness
Self-pity
Anger
Resentment

I am beginning to see it all now. The instant we are in a state of rebellion, we have not only lost our contentment and our joy; we have also declared personal war on God. If God is truly God, then He is Lord and Ruler of circumstances. So if we are rebellious against the circumstances He has allowed, then we are, in practical fact, rebelling against Him.

No wonder God withdrew His presence from me! My spirit of rebellion shuts the door in His face. It is saying, "I will do it my way from now on. I will be the boss of my own life."

Afterward, when the darkness descends and desolation overcomes one, a few halfhearted statements like, "Well, Lord, maybe I was a bit too self-confident . . . I guess I do need You after all . . . why don't we work out a sort of partnership?"—these little gestures won't restore the relationship. All-out repentance is needed.

So I'm having to go back to my childhood to try to locate the root of my rebellion against circumstances—and thus ultimately against God. I think it centered in the deprivation our family suffered during the Depression. Dad as a pastor of a small church made such a pitifully small income that we had but the barest essentials. I'll never forget the embarrassment of going with him to the market on Saturday and watching him whisper to the grocer, asking if he could receive credit until the first of the week.

I rebelled against our poverty, against the "missionary barrel" gifts of Dad's parishioners to our family, used and often soiled clothes that seldom fit properly. In college, my rebellion turned toward inequality of all kinds. Not having the right clothes for social affairs, I affected scorn for this part of college life. My non-acceptance of these situations never became serious enough to separate me from God back then, but seeds were sown—seeds of dissatisfaction, lack of gratitude. I'm having to search back through my life to each such occasion, confess the wrong spirit there, then ask the Lord's forgiveness.

I am beginning to look forward to these early morning times. There is an air of expectancy inside me as I watch the sun rise and wait for the Lord. What guidance will He give me today? Will it be a verse of Scripture? A hymn?

Today it was a poem:

> Awake my soul, and with the sun,
> Thy daily stage of duty run;
> Shake off dull sloth and joyful rise
> To pay the morning sacrifice!
>
> Shine on me, Lord, new life impart,
> Fresh ardors kindle in my heart;
> One ray of Thine all-quick'ning light
> Despite the clouds and dark of night.

Thomas Ken, 1637–1711

Thank You, Jesus, for revealing to me that to rise at six each morning is to travel from "dull sloth" to "fresh ardors." How glorious is the early morning air, the dazzling colors of the sunrise, the sweet bird sound, the fresh smell of the foliage and flowers!

Thank You, Lord, for the opportunity of this firsthand audience with the King. How privileged is that person who is admitted to Royal Presence, to listen to the almighty King, to watch Him, to bask in His majesty. In earthly courts, such a one would be considered favored indeed. Yet this is the status and the privilege You give to each of us, Lord.

This morning, Lord, I need to record my dream of last night. My dreams usually involve people and places. The one last night had neither, no pictures at all, only an idea. I don't believe I've ever had this kind of dream before.

The idea or thought was about You, Jesus. Not surprising, since I have felt closer and closer to You recently. The thought was about Your death on the cross. This was redemption for us, and You being who You are, God as well as man, insisted upon doing our redemption right, doing it to the last awful detail, all the way to the end. You could have taken so many shortcuts that would have made dying so much easier for You, *but You would not*.

And in my dream, as this realization swept over me, I wept.

The depths of meaning in this strange dream will be given me in time, I'm sure, because I'm convinced that it came from You. And how I rejoice that once more I have a relationship with You.

It was an example of a concept I received years ago from author-teacher-friend Glenn Clark: Prayers are answered and marvelous things happen when the unconscious and the conscious are of one piece and track perfectly together. What is tracking here—and how much this delights me!—is that the truth of Christianity is not just in my wide-awake mind, but deep down in my unconscious mind also.

Then You led me to these words:

Yes, even when I am old and gray-headed, O God, forsake me not, but keep me alive until I have declared Your mighty strength to this generation, and Your might and power to all that are to come.

Psalm 71:18, AMPLIFIED

Lord, I make this prayer for myself, that You will use me in the years ahead to *declare* You and Your works in a mighty way to this generation.

Changing _____

*L*en ... All of us rejoiced as the weeks passed and Catherine emerged from her isolation. There was a new softness in her demeanor. She laughed and joked more. My morning prayer time with her had a new vitality.

"What have you learned from all this?" I asked her one morning as the two of us ate breakfast together.

"Not to take myself so seriously," she replied with a smile. "I need to remind myself at least once a day that the world can get along just fine without me."

"How will all this affect your work?"

"I don't know yet. I'm not ready to begin a new book. Maybe later this year. I feel a great need to get myself better organized—papers, clothes, personal belongings. I need to give away a lot of things. The Lord has really zapped me about this."

Mary Moncur, our faithful housekeeper of many years, refilled our coffee cups. She was relaxed and smiling, too. During Catherine's long months of lethargy and moodiness, Mary had in some ways absorbed these attitudes into her small frame, trying to take the weight of Catherine's despair upon herself.

I felt lighter, too, somehow. It had been an extra strain to commute every other week to New York City, knowing my wife was going through a time of agonizing reappraisal of everything, including our marriage. Meanwhile, *Guideposts* magazine was entering a period of turbulent growth with more demands on my creativity. I sensed the time was approaching when I would have to make a hard decision as to whether I could continue as the full-time editor of a New York-based publication while living in Florida.

"Catherine, any revelation as to what got you into your— your dark state?"

An almost imperceptible shrug. "My usual overreacting and intensity, I guess. Also trying to play God with my family. The controlling mother syndrome, as my son would say."

"And being a perfectionist?"

"Yes, that fits."

"Do you think you're changing?"

Catherine tensed slightly. "I have always had high standards for myself and every member of our family. Even as a young girl I would listen to my father's sermons, knowing when his points were weak. I agonized when I felt he hadn't done his best.

"It was the same with Peter Marshall. He had a tremendous gift for communication, but I knew when he had not done enough preparation for a sermon. That's when I began to help him with research. I'm always straining for the best, in myself and in others. It hurts me when people do shoddy work. I tend to take it personally."

"I hope you never change, Catherine. Your quest for excellence shines through all your books. You get the absolute maximum from your talent. But how much can you—should you—transfer this to those close to you?"

"I know what you're getting at, Len. You think I'm too hard on Linda and Chester and Jeff."

"Yes, you're tough on them. More so than I. It used to bother me a lot. I didn't feel enough of your love went along with this toughness. I'm beginning to change my mind about this, however, and you need to know this."

"In what way, Len?"

"The past months have been a real learning time for me, too. In looking back at my first marriage, I see how I tried to smooth over the difficulties, rationalizing that I was a peacemaker. When his home situation is in chaos, a man tends to seek peace at any price. When you and the others pointed this out to me on Cape Cod last summer, I resisted it. But it's true. In my first marriage I now think I did damage to Eve by not confronting her more. I covered up for her too much, ducked the truth. If a father is obsessed with being a peacemaker, he tends to be overly permissive with his children. I thank God now for the way you came into our family of four confused, bruised individuals and set tough, high standards for every one of us."

Catherine's eyes teared up suddenly. "Len, you don't know how much this means to me. I've felt so guilty at times because I just couldn't manufacture the love I knew you wanted me to feel toward the children. I've never had a problem with your professional standards; I think you know how much I respect your editorial skills. I just hated to see your oh-so-casual approach to disciplining the children."

It was a beautiful moment at the breakfast table. I took her hand, then kissed her.

"I think I know what else you're thinking," Catherine said softly. "It concerns our marriage."

"Your perfectionism has made it difficult at times. My divorce, for example, is the essence of imperfection."

"That's true, Len. I wanted to ignore it, pretend it never happened. That was foolish of me. I let it fester inside."

"But God heals these wounds. He restores. He reconciles."

"I know that, and I'm struggling with all that right now. Forgive me for being the way I am. I can't seem to help it. I need to hear from the Lord. He is guiding me in so many ways now. I'm sure He'll give me His word about this, too."

Catherine . . . As Len and I continue to arise for worship each morning at 6 A.M. I do feel changes taking place inside me. Since I asked the Holy Spirit years ago to indwell me, then I conclude that He is at work, turning "bad" attitudes there into "good" ones.

Perhaps this is an analogy: It's as if the Spirit within me is the photographer's developing solution. By praising Him I have ceased fighting bad situations, so that these "negatives" can be bathed in the divine solution. Once bathed, the "negative" turns into the "positive"—black turns into white—and lo, we have a beautiful and acceptable picture.

Relinquishment is the key here. Certain evils (negatives) need to be turned over to God through praise so that He can work His powerful chemistry on them.

Paul told us, "Most gladly therefore will I rather glory in my infirmities" (2 Corinthians 12:9).

An "infirmity" can be interpreted as anything that bugs us persistently. For me, insomnia. It need not be a big thing, just something we live with day after day, but never seem to get on top of in our own strength. The healing can begin when we praise God for it. The words of a familiar hymn can start the process:

When morning gilds the skies,
My heart awaking cries,
May Jesus Christ be praised!
Alike at work and prayer,
To Jesus I repair;
May Jesus Christ be praised!

Tr. by Edward Caswall, 1814–1878

I was shaken this morning while reading the eleventh chapter of Paul's letter to the Romans. Three sins of which I have been guilty during the Amy Catherine ordeal:

(1) *Not trusting Jesus.* There was soul force in my determination that the Lord was going to heal Amy Catherine. I need to dig in on this: Why my almost frenzied take-charge attitude during those crucial days? *I did not trust Jesus.* I did not want anything but that the baby be completely healed. I was blind to the work Jesus was doing in the others: Pam, Linda, Jamie, Scott, Virginia, Len, and, of course, Peter and Edith.

(2) *Not valuing His grace.* I entered the Christian life by grace, but have had trouble living my life on that basis. Instead, I keep falling into the trap of thinking that being accepted and loved by Jesus depends on how I measure up. In turn, I relate to other people on the same basis.

Linda nailed me on this last summer. "Your love for me seems to depend on my performance. If I'm good there is acceptance; if I'm bad, rejection." All I can say to that is, "Ouch!"

(3) *Not abiding in His kindness.* What depths of meaning in the words *abiding* and *kindness!* Just the steadfast, constant love, the positive, simple, homespun kindness of Jesus. When will I learn to abide?

The ultimate statement of the inscrutability of God is made in these verses:

Oh, what a wonderful God we have! How great are his wisdom and knowledge and riches! How impossible it is for us to understand his decisions and his methods!

For who among us can know the mind of the Lord? Who knows enough to be his counselor and guide?

And who could ever offer to the Lord enough to induce him to act?

For everything comes from God alone. Everything lives by his power, and everything is for his glory. To him be glory evermore.

Romans 11:33–36, TLB

This morning I'm an hour late in getting up. Len is in New York. The temptation is to make it 7 A.M. from now on instead of 6. Would love that extra hour of sleep. What about this, Lord?

No answer. I guess I don't need an answer. The original word from Him stands. Starting at 7 A.M. cuts short my time with Him. I want You, Lord, more than I want sleep.

This morning before our prayer time I walked into the yard and over to the roses. An urge came over me to kneel in the dew-sparkled grass and bury my nose in the flowers' fragrance. My heart seemed to explode with, "Thank You, Lord, for such beauty! Oh, how it feeds my spirit!"

In my devotion times I find my mind still coming up with verses from old hymns. What a treasure lies in great words that have been sung millions of times by millions of people! What healing power!

Often just a single line of an old hymn will come to mind. I write it down and wait to see if the Holy Spirit gives me the whole verse. Sometimes He does. If not, I search out the rest of the words in my collection of old hymnbooks.

There is therapy in this for me, because as I look through these old hymnals additional verses jump out at me. I sit down and read them over and over. God is planting them in me to help my spirit grow. Like this one:

> My hope is built on nothing less
> Than Jesus' blood and righteousness;
> I dare not trust the sweetest frame,
> But wholly lean on Jesus' name.
>
> [Refrain:] On Christ, the solid rock, I stand;
>   All other ground is sinking sand,
>   All other ground is sinking sand.
>
> When darkness veils His lovely face
> I rest on His unchanging grace;
> In every high and stormy gale,
> My anchor holds within the veil.

Edward Mote, 1797–1874

I underlined the words *When darkness veils His lovely face I rest on His unchanging grace.* Here are the words that fill my cup. I need to repeat them over and over until they are deep in my unconscious. Then when the next crisis, or time of darkness, or merely His silence, comes, I have something to draw upon.

It is raining this morning, so Len and I are inside listening to the raindrops pelt our roof. We need the rain, Lord, so thank You for the moisture that will sink into the earth and nourish our flowers and fruit trees.

Gratitude wells up inside me, Lord, that Your Spirit, too, is sinking into me, Your words nourishing the roots of my being.

Here's a song I haven't sung in years. It spells out exactly how my spirit is being revived:

> For the beauty of the earth,
> For the glory of the skies,
> For the love which from our birth

Over and around us lies:
Lord of all, to Thee we raise
This our hymn of grateful praise.

Folliott S. Pierpoint, 1835–1917

A feeling rises up inside me that little trickles of praise are now running together, merging, beginning to form a small river of praise. It began mechanically, yet now has increasingly the feel of spontaneous emotion.

Slowly but surely my mind is being cleansed. Rich, beautiful, positive words are taking over, chasing away the negative ones. I am being filled with Your light.

Lord Jesus, how radiant and glorious is that light of Yours! Yesterday afternoon You gave me a glimpse of Your Kingdom that I cannot reflect on even now without tears of gratitude.

I was seated in a chair in the living room alone, thinking about all that I have been learning these past few months. I did not fall asleep, so this was not a dream. Nor was it an ethereal, other-worldly "vision." It seemed real, as real as the fabric on the chair, or the Florida sunlight pouring through the windows, or the trilling of a mockingbird in a ficus tree outside. Suddenly I felt the living presence of Jesus. What joy to have this again in my life!

"We're going on a journey," You told me.

Soon we were in what seemed to be a large and impressive throne room. Crowds of people lined the walls on all sides. As we walked the length of the room approaching One whom I knew to be God the Father, I spotted in the crowd those I love who had gone on before: my father; Peter Marshall; my grandson, Peter Christopher—now not a baby, but a curly-haired five-year-old. Crawling delightedly about his feet was a bright-eyed one-year-old I recognized as Amy Catherine.

Then I looked down at myself. To my horror I was dressed in rags—torn, unwashed, filthy. How could I bear to stand before the Father, the Lord God omnipotent, clothed so vilely? When we stopped before the Throne, I could not even look up. I had never felt so unworthy.

In the same instant, Lord Jesus, You spread wide the voluminous robe You were wearing, completely covering me with it. "Now," You told me, "My Father does not see you at all, only Me. Not your sins but My righteousness. I cover for you."

Then I was aware again of the living room and the chair where I had been sitting—and of inexpressible joy and gratitude washing over me.

Sleep _____

*C*atherine . . . That magnificent "journey in the spirit" last week prompts me to step out in greater faith and trust. It is time to confront an old enemy—sleeplessness. My remedy for this in the past has been sleeping pills. And even these do not always work. I've gone through a real agony of spirit about this.

Finally, before I went to sleep the night before last, I was promised that Jesus would speak to me regarding this. He did. It happened while I was standing before the kitchen sink last evening after dinner.

"Do it [ditch the pills] for love of Me. Sleep is probably your most cherished possession. Therefore, lay your cherished possession on the altar. Make this your alabaster box of ointment poured out for Me."

I had already, that afternoon, promised Him that I would do whatever He asked—so, of course, I will. It's one of the biggest steps I have ever taken.

This is a day to praise God. For I did it: flushed the sleeping pills, more than $50 worth of them, down the john. Then I spent two hours trying to sleep yesterday afternoon, just lying there on the cot in my study, tossing and turning in a state of inner terror. Of what I do not know.

It's been a week of sleepless nights, exhausted days—and always that nameless fear. I prayed about it and the answer came: "Make a list of the *positive* things you accomplished last week."

I did so, a good list of steps taken, drawers cleaned, clothes given away, and so on. My mind tends to veer off on another track, however, thinking of the long, wakeful hours, resenting the fact that God has not rushed immediately to my rescue during these torturous times. But then the counter-insight comes: "I want to do more than handle your sleep problem. You're demanding an instant miracle in one area. I want a healing of the whole woman."

This will undoubtedly include things undreamed of at this moment. But I do know that it will include a real cleansing of my subconscious. So much debris, so much negativism, so many fear thoughts, so many thoughts of *nonacceptance by God* have piled up.

Tomorrow will be the one-week anniversary of this pill-dumping adventure. But because I've slept so little during this time, it seems more like a month.

Last night was the worst night of all when I was truly desperate and in tears. This morning the Holy Spirit dropped a single phrase into my mind: *Blessed assurance, Jesus is mine. . . .*

I recognized it as the beginning of the old Gospel hymn. I went to my hymnal and reviewed the rest of the lines:

> *Blessed assurance, Jesus is mine!*
> *O what a foretaste of glory divine!*
> *Heir of salvation, purchase of God,*
> *Born of His Spirit, washed in His blood.*
> *This is my story, this is my song,*
> *Praising my Saviour all the day long;*
> *This is my story, this is my song,*
> *Praising My Saviour all the day long.*

Fanny J. Crosby, 1820–1915

After singing these words several times, I understood the Holy Spirit's message: *Settle down to knowing that you are accepted by the Father, by Jesus, and by Me. Be assured of Our love. Rest in it.*

After another night of sleeplessness these words from the 121st psalm:

> My help cometh from the Lord,
> which made heaven and earth.
> He will not suffer thy foot to be moved:
> *he that keepeth thee will not slumber.*

verses 2–3

How comforting to know that God never sleeps in His watchfulness over us. If we are awake, so is He, never wearying in His constant care. And another thought this morning: As long as I "battle" for sleep, it will not come. For sleep must be essentially a giving-up process and my releasing myself to it.

Lord, this morning I am astonished and delighted with the variety of words You bring to my mind, songs and

poems I memorized years ago but thought I had forgotten.
Here is the verse You gave me today:

> O God, I cried, no dark disguise
>   can e'er hereafter hide from me
> Thy radiant identity!
> Thou canst not move across the grass
> But my quick eye will see Thee pass,
> Nor speak, however silently,
> But my hushed voice will answer Thee.
> I know the path that tells Thy way
> Through the cool eve of every day;
> God, I can push the grass apart
> And lay my fingers on Thy heart.

Renascence, Edna St. Vincent Millay, 1892–1950

Lord, You are indeed a "radiant identity"!

This morning I must deal with a prophecy I received
some time ago in my prayer group. I confess my reluctance
to follow through on it. It was that I must allow myself to be
"hid with Christ in God" (Colossians 3:3). I read about this
admonition years ago in one of Hannah Whitall Smith's
books, and avoided it then, too. I must have been afraid it
would mean my being wiped out—that if I were "hid with
Christ," I, as a person, would be no more.

Today I'm convicted. For what my reluctance means, of
course, is that I want the world to see me, not Jesus.

So I confess to You this morning my divided will on this.
You know how much I have loved being with You, talking
and listening. But I confess that I find being hid completely
by Your cloak and Your personality difficult. I've enjoyed
the world's acclaim, reveled in my "own" success. This
desire to be noticed and admired has been going on since I
was a teenager—and before.

So will You take the part of my will that still wants "fame

and fortune" in this world and tame that kicking child part of me? Will You make me all of one piece so that I'm willing, even eager, to be hid with and in You? I hereby not only give You permission to do this, but I ask You to do it.

And I do now—by faith and with gratitude—accept the forgiveness and the "hiddenness" that You held out to me in that vision of Your Throne room.

Thank You that when I am hid with You, standing before the mercy seat of the Father, it is a Throne of mercy and not of judgment.

Thank You that You, Lord Jesus, are willing to—and do—stand for me before the Father, so that He does not see my sins and failures at all, but only You.

Thank You for hiddenness. Make it complete and lasting, so that the sweet freedom of forgiveness will be lasting, too.

Following my confession of last week about my reluctance to be "hid with Christ," I had an extraordinary Communion experience today in church. In a moment of pure faith and illumination, I was able to take the bread and wine, believing that Jesus Himself, His physical body, His attributes, the essence of His being, were flowing into me, was becoming an integral part of me. During that exhilarating moment I was truly lost in Him.

The fact that I had said yes to Him last week in an all-out assent of my will must have made it possible. In thinking back through the years, I have said yes to Him many times. I see now that this is the way it must be, given our egotistical natures, bending our will to Him over and over.

This morning I'm grappling with an old enemy, fear. Just when I seem to be winning one battle, something else happens to defeat me.

I've tried to keep my mind on You, Jesus, praising You for the renewal of our relationship. Then I keep feeling this lump on my right side. It has been there for over a month now. The doctor isn't much concerned, seems to think it's just fatty tissue. "If it doesn't go away in a few months, come back and we'll look at it again," he told me.

Len and I have prayed about it, but it hasn't gone away. Now I'm battling perhaps the oldest enemy I have.

All my life I seem to have had a problem with fear. My mind goes back to the sessions Peter, Edith, Len, and I had last summer on the Cape, trying to trace the roots of fear back through the generations. Clearly we got only a start with this.

This morning I keep repeating over and over again, "Faith overcomes fear." That has helped. Then I focus on this verse, repeating it over and over:

> For God hath not given us the spirit of fear; but of power, and of love, and of a sound mind.
>
> 2 Timothy 1:7, KJV

The Writer _____

*C*atherine . . . It is almost 8 A.M., Lord, and I seem to have fallen back into the pit again. Len is in New York and I've had a miserable night. It must have been 4 A.M. before I fell asleep. Then I slept through my 6 A.M. rising alarm.

The main reason for my heaviness this morning is my manuscript *Gloria*. It has had more lives than a cat. I've buried it and then resurrected it so many times.

Recently I gave it a new look as a nonfiction book, a suggestion from an editor at *Guideposts*. Len was skeptical because of Gloria's unpredictable marriage situation. But I spent several weeks doing resuscitation work.

At 5 P.M. yesterday, I telephoned Gloria and for a few minutes chatted with her about the project. Then came the bombshell: "Catherine, my present plan is to go ahead and use the new no-fault Florida divorce law to terminate my marriage. I won't be accepting any engagements after the first of the year because I know how some Christians feel about divorce. But the marriage is over."

So after four years' work, endless hours of recorded interviewing, and the expense of transcribing all that—300-plus pages of manuscript written in three versions—this time we tell *Gloria* goodbye and finally bury her. Once again others have been right, while I've been wrong.

Lord, I need help to get over this death!

Another factor in my spiritual decline this past week is this lump in my side. Yesterday Len and I went to see the doctor about it. He said that if I had to have a lump in my body, this was the kind to have, a cyst in the fatty tissue. Once again he said he thought it harmless. But of course, he added, you never know for sure until you operate. He suggests I have it removed as a hospital outpatient under a local anesthetic.

I am puzzled as to why with all our praying about this, we have not been able to get it dissolved or absorbed by prayer. It's apparently not a big problem in any case. Doctors consider it about on a par with having wisdom teeth cut out. So far, the only word from the Lord I've been able to hear is that it does not matter in this instance whether I rely on doctors or not. By which He, too, must be telling me that the cyst is harmless.

Yet it is a negative that weighs down my spirit.

This morning I am back again at my 6 A.M. arising. Last week when I repeatedly flunked the 6 A.M. test, nothing went right. I need this morning time with You, Lord. These words now penetrate my darkness, but I do not know the source:

Thank You, Lord Jesus,
for the mysterious mind of man
that can think
and retain memories,
that can plan ahead
and question
and put ideas together—
new with old, for that is creativity.
Thank You for the beating of my heart,
so that I am still alive on this earth;
for the mysterious mechanism of breathing;
for ears to hear the birds
trilling their greeting to
the morning outside my window.
Thank You for darkness that turns into day.

Special words, Lord, as I begin all over again to learn how to praise You and trust in You.

I'm beginning to understand why it is so important that I begin my recovery period early in the morning with praise. There is a progression here that I'm slowly perceiving.

First, the time of day is crucial. In the early morning we are freshest in body, mind, and spirit. There is the freshness of the day itself. It is quiet. Fewer distractions and voices to jam the wavelengths between us and the Lord.

Jesus always seemed to be up and about early in the morning. It was His favorite time. He sets the pattern for us.

Second, I'm discovering that praise is the only valid taking-off point for prayer. We have to establish the connection between us and the Lord before we can ask Him for anything in faith. Only worship can establish this connection. And worship begins with praise—praise that focuses our attention on the beauty and love and saving power of Jesus.

I'm indebted to the Holy Spirit for teaching me this. He did it through bringing to life for me one of those little vignettes or snapshots tucked into the pages of the New Testament. This one was of the time Jesus and His disciples sought overnight lodging in a Samaritan village and were turned away. When His disciples asked Jesus to bring down the fire of heaven upon these villagers, He rebuked them:

> "You do not know what manner of spirit you are of. For the Son of Man did not come to destroy men's lives but to save them."
>
> Luke 9:55–56, NKJ

I've recently been in the same mood as Jesus' apostles. My "righteous" indignation has been directed toward the officials of a church who have been most insensitive in dealing with a troubled woman.

Then the Spirit led me to that story in Luke. Such gratitude rose in me that Jesus never falls into the negative traps we do! Always and always He remains the Savior, staying immovably on the saving side—always constructive, always upbeat, always creative. No wonder He is the only One worthy of our worship!

In the days that followed I had only to let my spiritual eyes glimpse this snapshot again, and the praise would rise. In turn I discovered what a boost this gave to faith. Small prayer requests were answered during those days grounded in praise. There would be throughout the day the delicious feeling of no out-of-jointness, of my life all in alignment.

Third, the Holy Spirit showed me that I was constantly being trapped by one of Satan's oldest tricks: looking at the problem instead of at Jesus and His power. I had listened, really paid attention to Old Scratch's suggestions, for example, as to how difficult it would be for me to get going again on another book after the *Gloria* fiasco. I got to thinking that this was going to be the most difficult prayer God ever had to answer. The reasons *why* I couldn't do it seemed so massive, so logical.

The Comforter told me that all of this had been Satan's technique for discouraging me unduly and that I must *never* fall for this temptation again. Here again, it is my joyful praise that thwarts the enemy and negates his sly suggestions.

The Spirit of Control _____

*Y*ou have been speaking to me, Lord, about my children and grandchild. In the early morning times You have been showing me quite firmly that *they are not mine but Yours.* You love them far more than I ever could. You loaned them to me for a season. Now I am to take my possessive, managing hands off—strictly off.

This is never easy for me. I have tried to be involved in my son Peter's life and family. Peter and Edith resist this, though sometimes they need me and call for me, as they did a year ago with the Amy Catherine crisis. But I see now I went too far in that situation; took too much of the burden onto myself; even presumed to assign blame for the outcome, deciding that Amy Catherine's death was Peter and Edith's fault for allowing the liver biopsy, or the result of the group's lack of singleminded prayer power. God has shown me unmistakably over the past year that He is sovereign over our flawed nature!

When I first became stepmother to Linda, Chester, and Jeff, I did not have the love for them that I did for my own flesh and blood. But a surprising thing has happened the past few months. I feel myself yearning for a closer relationship with each of them. This is Your doing, Lord.

The other morning came the crowning touch. I was reading in the Psalms when suddenly these words leapt from the page:

> The Lord will perfect that which concerneth me: thy mercy, O Lord, endureth for ever: forsake not the works of thine own hands.
>
> Psalm 138:8, KJV

I could—and did—claim this promise promptly and with such rejoicing! You will perfect my children and grandchildren in Your way and in Your timing. Years ago You began this work. It is Your business to complete what You start. You have promised that You will. I've claimed and accepted this promise. It's as good as done. My heart is rejoicing. Weights and weights have been lifted from me.

Today this verse is given to me:

> . . . God who began the good work within you will keep right on helping you grow in his grace until his task within you is finally finished.
>
> Philippians 1:6, TLB

And to top it off, the Holy Spirit is reminding me that "Jesus is the Author and Finisher of our faith." Of course! The Finisher!

Praising You is the key to letting You get on with the job.

I need to record here how my morning times of praise have opened my heart in a new way. The Lord has been leading me to certain passages of Scripture to teach me things about myself that in the past I have not wanted to hear.

One of the most quoted sections of Scripture is the thirteenth chapter of 1 Corinthians. I have not wanted to face up to the truth it expresses:

> Charity suffereth long, and is kind; charity envieth not; charity vaunteth not itself, is not puffed up, doth not behave itself unseemly, seeketh not her own, is not easily provoked, thinketh no evil; rejoiceth not in iniquity, but rejoiceth in the truth; beareth all things, believeth all things, hopeth all things, endureth all things. Charity never faileth. . . .
>
> 1 Corinthians 13:4–8, KJV

Perhaps the biggest point of contention between Len and me in twelve years of marriage has been my unloving attitude toward Linda. I knew I was in the wrong here. God pointed it out to me early in our marriage when we were living in Chappaqua. Because Linda was willful and stubborn (qualities I recognize in myself), I became judgmental toward her.

Then came that memorable moment in the Chappaqua Congregational Church so many years ago. The winter sunlight was coming through the tall windows. I even remember that we were sitting on the right side of the church. The Spirit said so clearly, *If you can't love Linda, you can't love Me.*

A devastating statement! Queer about love . . . is it then of one piece, so that when we deliberately withhold it from any single human being, we deny love itself and, in the end, are rendered incapable of loving?

My attitude about Linda during her early teens was—all right, Lord, since You say I must, I'll go on forgiving her for her deception and for her poor grades that, to me, were incomprehensible for a girl with an IQ of 169. I would forgive her, but love her? Impossible! We can't manufacture love, can we? Toleration and politeness were as far as I could go.

The real problem here, of course, was my will. I wasn't willing to let God give me the gift of love for Linda, or to let Him love her through me.

Many times I've asked myself, What's behind the inability of a parent to love a stepchild? It's widespread in our society, and as divorces multiply, it becomes an increasing problem. I've heard experts on family life talk about stepmother/stepdaughter relationships as though there is almost a chemical factor here that causes jealousy, resentment, friction. It's been said that different generations are always in understandable conflict. And that whenever two broken families are merged, relationship problems are inevitable.

I'm sure there is truth in all this, but that does not let me off the hook. The Spirit of God can work miracles in all these situations. He has shown me that my arrogance and pride in my own opinions go hand-in-hand with my being a very *controlling* person. That means that I try to play God with husband, son, stepchildren, other relatives, even with friends. So highly do I regard my convictions, pet theories, and tastes that when anyone resists them, I become angry and resentful, even to the point of turning against that person.

This is what happened between Linda and me. I really had not wanted to do anything about it until a year ago on Cape Cod. A start was made when I confessed to her my "elder brother" attitude and we hugged each other. But it was only a beginning.

Now the Spirit is showing me that this root of bitterness toward Linda, no matter how much I went through the motions of forgiving her and releasing her from my judgment, was poisoning other relationships—especially with Len. Nay, even more it was rendering me incapable of loving anyone, even the Lord Himself.

Charity endureth all things. That spells it all out for me. So in Len's presence—the Lord stressed that I was to do this with him—I got down on my knees this morning, confessed all this, and asked God to give me the gift of love for Linda. I don't know how or exactly when He will achieve this, but achieve it He will. Nothing could be more in line with His will.

The Spirit is continuing to teach me about control. I need to understand, for example, the difference between the parental authority that is approved—established—by God, and the tendency we have to dominate our children in the wrong way.

I can see that when parents have a *spirit of control,* our children feel this and react against it, even when they haven't consciously analyzed the problem. A case in point is Jeff and the advice I gave him (in a spirit of control) regarding his choice of courses this year in prep school. He resisted some of my suggestions and I reacted emotionally rather than objectively.

The Spirit pointed me back to the years of my girlhood in Keyser, West Virginia. I was undoubtedly a peculiar, introspective child, not a good mixer, lacking in social graces. In the early grades I got my satisfaction from proving how superior I was in schoolwork, pulling down excellent grades. When I was a teenager, while others were beginning to date, my lack of social adjustment became more obvious.

It was to this period that the Spirit pointed me. He asked

me to repent of the way I had justified my lack of popularity by retreating even further into my "superiority."

So this morning I've had to renounce the lie that I ever was, or ever will be, "superior" to anybody. Then I was told to accept and embrace the truth that of myself I have no value, that what I achieve or what I amount to depends on the degree that Jesus is allowed to live in me and work through me.

What the Spirit showed me is almost a lifetime of the Pharisaical attitude: "Lord, I thank Thee that I am not as other men." No wonder I have been super-critical and judgmental! No wonder I have sought to be controlling! No wonder I have not been able to express love to others.

Len has a constant hunger to get close to me, to see into my thoughts, to have a deep togetherness. I have resisted this because I have always been a solitary person.

The other morning when I was being shown that I not only had to be willing to love Linda but to be more open to Len, I wanted to make this confession to Jesus alone. But Jesus said, "No, do this before Len. You have to begin to make your prayers *real*. There's no other way except the kind of honesty that bares your soul to another human being."

When I did, it was not as difficult as I anticipated. Afterward, I felt as if I had had a spiritual bath and cleansing.

Now this morning, in retrospect, I have further insight about this: If I will continue to make my prayers real in this way, the glimpses this will give Len into my innermost heart will supply him the emotional satisfaction of togetherness that he so craves. Has not my ghastly sense of superiority, even toward Len, resulted in my wanting my "real" communications with Jesus alone, thus making my prayers with Len shallow and phony, and shutting him out? He has felt this deeply and reacted with resentment.

Could it even be that one of the reasons Jesus withdrew Himself from me was to force me into a closer relationship with Len?

Relinquishment _____

*V*irginia Lively ... In the spring of 1972 my daughter Linda called me with wonderful news. She was fairly bubbling over the phone. "Mom, know what my problem has been all these years? Low blood sugar. I can do something about that!".

I was overjoyed. It was the answer to my prayer on the beach that morning on Cape Cod six months earlier. All those years Linda had had a severe case of hypoglycemia. How well I remembered scolding her for eating nothing but doughnuts and a cola drink for breakfast! Now, as she began drinking milk (which she'd always hated), cutting out sweets, and eating balanced meals, her mysterious symptoms disappeared, one by one, until she was completely healed.

Lord, when I placed Linda's healing in Your hands—and took my own anxious ones off—how swiftly and sovereignly You acted!

Catherine . . . I have something else to praise God for this morning. After waiting and hoping for months now that the lump in my side would dissolve, and after bombarding it daily with prayer, yesterday I went to the doctor for surgery. The lump was removed in a simple and painless procedure. The fatty tissue was examined and found not to be malignant.

This morning I also began using my concordance to trace the words *light* and *darkness* in Scripture. In the process came the discovery that God uses both for His purposes:

> I form the light and create darkness. . . .
>
> Isaiah 45:7, NIV
>
> He made darkness his covering, his canopy around him. . . .
>
> Psalm 18:11, NIV
>
> If I say, "Surely the darkness will hide me and the light become night around me," even the darkness will not be dark to you; the night will shine like the day, for darkness is as light to you.
>
> Psalm 139:11–12, NIV

As I arise early each morning for praise and prayer, the "dark" of my experience is revealed as God's loving provision, just as much as the days spent in the sunshine of His blessing.

Reading Agnes Sanford this morning about the drama of the Garden of Eden, and Adam and Eve being required by their Creator *not* to eat of the tree of the knowledge of good and evil, has started a train of thought in my mind. . . .

The food we eat provides the building blocks out of which the tissues of our body are made. In the same way, what we "eat" via our thought and imaginative life provides the building blocks out of which our souls and spirits are built. They are either nourished and grown in the knowledge and love of God, or else they atrophy and die.

God means for us to look at the good, the beautiful, the true, the pure.

But how can we do that when all about us in the world is full of evil and pain?

The answer Agnes Sanford gives confirms what I've been learning elsewhere these past months: Learn to look steadily at Jesus Christ. Jesus points out to her the areas of the world—the issues or persons—about which He wants her to pray on a given day. Then not only does He keep her informed of all that she needs to know about these particular situations (thus becoming for her the knowledge of good and evil), but also this knowledge does not depress her mind or hurt her body in the way the continual absorption of evil tidings across the board can hurt the rest of us. Agnes Sanford is doing something constructive about specific evils rather than simply bemoaning and wallowing in negatives.

The Lord is teaching me something every day about myself. Some of it has been painful. I see ever more clearly how off-the-track I was in the summer of '71, wanting to play God with Amy Catherine, rather than take the lower seat at the banquet table (Luke 14:7–11) and watch God in action.

Now the clear insight comes to me that the undying ember underneath my guilt over marrying a divorced man is not so much that I disobeyed one of God's laws (no such lofty remorse), but rather that I have set for myself the God-playing role of always having to be right. I keep giving an order to myself subconsciously that I must never make a mistake with a major decision. It's really sheer egotism all the way. What an insight! Lord, thank You. What a fool this mortal has been.

Back to my childhood again. I must be the best. I must get top grades. I must win debates and prizes for speaking. I must never be wrong. This has been my bondage ever since. Those areas like sports and popularity, in which I couldn't be tops—those I left strictly alone.

Then this insight: The true definition of a fanatic is one who is playing God in some arena of life—political, medical, educational, theological, relational. He is certain that his ideas and stand are necessary to "salvation" in his particular domain.

What happens is that Satan hoodwinks all of us terribly sincere folk through his age-old trick of tempting us to act as gods, the sin as old as Lucifer of usurping God's place. This, of course, leads to all kinds of excess, taking oneself too seriously, coming to believe that one is indispensable. Thank You, Lord, for exposing me as one of these misguided fanatics.

Len and I had been trying to find a time to be with Tom and Debby, a young couple having trouble in their marriage. I contacted Debby by phone; she suggested Saturday morning. I had a conflict, so we came up with Sunday afternoon, if it checked out with Len.

"Is Sunday afternoon okay to meet with Tom and Debby?" I asked him.

Len grimaced. "Not good for me."

"Why not?"

"There's a football game on TV I want to see."

"You put a TV program ahead of ministry?"

Len looked uncomfortable. He had constantly made the

point with our children that any TV-watching came second to activities in which they participated in person, such as family outings, sports, or church events.

"Don't Tom and Debby have any other time free?" he asked me.

Now I was on the defensive. "Yes. Saturday morning."

"That's fine with me."

"Well, it's not for me."

"Why not?"

"I have a date to get my hair fixed."

"You put a hairdo ahead of ministry?"

It really was funny, only neither of us was laughing. Len had often accused me of giving my hair too great a priority. He had no understanding of how we women feel about such things. So we glowered at each other, ending up seeing Tom and Debby Sunday evening.

Later that still, small voice said, *Ask Len why he has such resentment about your hair appointments.*

I did. He responded with vigorous denials of any resentment. As we talked I realized that my hair appointments were not the issue. Our relationship for the past few years was the issue. The Lord was trying to tell me something here.

As a result I've begun praying harder for answers to my questions about our marriage.

One morning soon afterward, Len and I were sitting up in bed having our morning prayer together, when out of Len's mouth came an insight, a word that was clearly not his at all, but the Lord's.

I cannot recall the exact words Len spoke, but the essence was this: "In every onward step in the Christian's life, you can only come to the Lord as you are. You learn that first in connection with salvation itself. It's the same with each subsequent step, because everything you receive from God is a gift—unearned, solely by grace."

This spoke directly to my current concern with Christian growth. But the further lesson for me was: *God had spoken through Len.* Clearly, God was saying to me through this: "Your criticism of Len has been off-base and displeasing to me. It's the same spirit that Michal had when she looked down on King David [2 Samuel 6:16]. It's dangerous to your spirit. Cut it out."

Then this dream the other night. In it several of the stones had come out of the engagement ring Len gave me before our marriage thirteen years ago. I was sifting through a box half-filled with sand and bits of debris, hunting for the diamonds and the sapphire that is the center stone. At last I located the gems.

The next morning as I was pondering the dream, I reached these conclusions: Despite the debris in our lives, God has brought good out of our marriage and will continue to do so. More pinpointedly, marriage to Len might well be God's tailor-made human situation to correct what is wrong in me.

Thus as I recognize God's hand in our marriage (and I have increasingly resisted this during the past few years), I am now able to praise Him more genuinely and enthusiastically for my situation. This darkness, too, will be turned into light.

New Life _____

Catherine . . . This morning, Lord, I need to be with You, listen to Your words, drink in Your wisdom. So much has happened to me recently that I can hardly absorb it all. I know now that You didn't leave me during that long, dark period last year. You withdrew for a while to let me grow up a bit.

In a few days I'll be sixty years old. Some months ago I faced this milestone with gloom and foreboding. I was like those melancholy men who came to see me after Peter Marshall's death and told me that my financial picture was very bad, that I would have to sell the house, the car, and find a job in an office somewhere. I was 34 then and refused to accept this verdict. Instead I began to put together a book of Peter Marshall's sermons. This gave God an opportunity to activate in me His gift of writing. This launched a new career—and a new life—for me.

Today I hear You saying that as of right now I'm to stop playing the role of those gloomy men who put limits on what God can do in my situation. God is telling me that I am poised on the edge of another new life now at age sixty just as surely as I was at 34. "Believe in it," He says. "Believe in Me. Open your eyes and see My invisible chariots standing all around you to rescue you and move you on your new way."

This morning I can feel my next writing project groping for its deep roots, thrusting down in search of the life-giving water at some deep level in my being. Bit by bit, stroke by stroke, I watch the chapters emerging on such subjects as praise, forgiveness, healing, the move of the Holy Spirit.

The creative process is a little like the bulbs one plants that must begin their growth in the dark for a time. Even the formation of the earth began in *darkness*. What a different perspective this puts on the dark night I've so recently emerged from. For the first time I'm beginning to understand how the saints could praise God for this experience!

I've shared this project with Len, who is enthusiastic and has already come up with a title for the book: *Something More.*

November 30, 1973 . . . Unexpected news from Edith and Peter! Edith is pregnant and expecting a baby next May. We'd understood that in view of the heartaches with Peter Christopher and Amy Catherine, they'd decided not to try again. And they did not. This pregnancy is strictly un-planned; neither Peter nor Edith can figure out when con-ception took place. Thus, how else can we take this except as an "act of God"?

May 4, 1974 ... Last Saturday at about three in the afternoon Peter Jonathan Marshall was born. Weight: eight pounds, thirteen ounces. I have never heard Peter so excited as he was over the telephone. "Mom, you have a grandson! He's normal. Perfect." Praise God! How can we find words in the English language adequate to express our joy and thanksgiving?

Jonathan means "gift of God."

God knew that if this baby had been defective, there was no fight left in us. It would have been too much for us to bear.

I've never heard Edith so bubbly and happy as when she described the baby. As she studies his little face, she sees features and characteristics of all the children, especially the two deceased babies. She reports that he has Peter Christopher's beautifully shaped head and chin; Amy Catherine's mouth; Mary Elizabeth's large eyes. It's as if God is saying, "See, I am giving you all the babies in one beautiful, perfect baby."

At his church service the day after Peter Jonathan was born, Peter read these selections from the 66th psalm:

> You have purified us with fire, O Lord, like silver in a crucible. You captured us in your net and laid great burdens on our backs. You sent troops to ride across our broken bodies. We went through fire and flood. But in the end, you brought us into wealth and great abundance.
>
> Now I have come to your Temple with burnt-offerings to pay my vows. . . .
>
> Come and hear, all of you who reverence the Lord, and I will tell you what he did for me. For I cried to him for help, with praises ready on my tongue. He would not have listened if I had not confessed my sins. But He listened! He heard my prayer! He paid attention to it!
>
> Blessed be God who didn't turn away when I was praying, and didn't refuse me his kindness and love.
>
> Psalm 66:10–20, TLB

September 24, 1980 ... Another joyous family event—
David Christopher Marshall was born to Peter and Edith;
weight, nine pounds, three ounces. Normal and healthy in
every respect.

It was Virginia Lively who heard this message: *This
child will not live. But any other child they have they may
have in perfect confidence.*

Thank You, Lord, for blessing our family so richly.

Afterword _____

*L*en . . . Catherine came out of her dark night experience with greater maturity and a new creativity. The result was a flow of articles, books, and teachings on the deeper walk. Her books published in the next ten years would include *Something More, Adventures in Prayer, The Helper, Meeting God at Every Turn,* and the novel *Julie.*

The experience was life-changing for me, too, in several ways. In 1974, after much internal agony and struggle, I listened to the Lord about a career change. Trying to be the full-time editor of *Guideposts* while living in Florida was hurting my marriage, making me a divided person, and shortchanging the magazine.

After 28 years at *Guideposts*, I resigned and waited for God to guide me. He did—into Christian book publishing. Catherine and I became partners with John and Elizabeth Sherrill of a company we named Chosen Books, which went on to publish most of the titles listed above, plus other bestsellers like *The Hiding Place*, *Born Again*, and *Life Sentence*.

In addition to writing regular articles for *Guideposts* up to the time of her death in 1983, Catherine and I jointly taught a class on the Christian walk for seven years at our Presbyterian church in Delray Beach, Florida. Later, with Pastor George Callahan, the two of us helped start the New Covenant Presbyterian Church in Pompano Beach, Florida.

Then in 1979 Catherine was given a vision by the Lord for an intercessory prayer ministry, with this instruction: *There is a great untapped reservoir of people who have the heart for intercession and are not being used. Call them into service.*

This prayer ministry was launched by Catherine and me in 1980 as *The Intercessors*, a part of the nonprofit *Breakthrough*. Today we have nearly 2,000 intercessors mobilized to pray for the needs of people whose letters pour into our office by the hundreds each week. A bimonthly teaching newsletter on intercession goes out to 15,000 prayer partners. (One may receive it without charge by writing to Breakthrough, Lincoln, VA 22078.)

During the last year of Catherine's life, as she was in and out of the hospital, there was a constant flow of family members to her side. It brought tears to my eyes the way Catherine reached out to Linda. The healing between them was complete, the love bonded in eternity.

Catherine and I had rejoiced in 1980 when Linda married Philip Lader, a man with special skills in law and business whose speaking gift reminded Catherine of Peter Marshall, Sr. Both Linda and Phil wanted children, yet years passed without a pregnancy.

Then there was our last visit to the Lader home in Hilton Head Island. One morning after Phil had left for work, Catherine received guidance that she, Linda, and I were to kneel by the Lader bed and pray that a conception would take place—in that very bed.

In March 1983 Catherine passed away. When Phil was named president of Winthrop College two months later, the Laders rented out their Hilton Head home and moved to Rock Hill, South Carolina. Soon Linda, as the president's wife only twelve years after her own college experience, was amazing me with her poise and organizational skills as she served as a hostess and model to young people on campus.

On February 2, 1985, Linda and Phil called me with great elation to announce that their first child had just been born: Mary Catherine Lader, named after Phil's mother and Catherine.

Catherine, not only do you have a namesake, but as it turns out, Mary Catherine was conceived on a visit back to Hilton Head, in the very bed you prayed over!

On June 17, 1987, a sister was born to Mary Catherine—Linda Whitaker Lader—Whitaker for Catherine's mother, Leonora Whitaker (Christy) Wood. Leonora passed away quietly and beautifully in her sleep on February 19, 1989, at the age of 97.

In August 1980 Chester married Susan Scott, a talented interior designer and tennis player he met while he was a student at McCallie School, a prep school for boys in Chattanooga, Tennessee. On May 8, 1981, Jacob Leonard LeSourd was born; on September 18, 1983, his sister, Hadley Johnson LeSourd entered the world.

At the time of Catherine's death Chester was an English

teacher and tennis coach at McCallie. In a moving and
memorable talk in the school chapel, Chet honored Catherine for her tough but prayer-centered discipline. "It was
the best possible launch pad I could have into adult life," he
told the teenage boys.

In October 1986 Jeffrey married Nancy Oliver, a partner
in a Washington, D.C., law firm. Jeff opened the marriage
ceremony by paying an unusual tribute to his stepmother.
He told the church packed with friends and family that it
had been his dream as a boy that Catherine would live long
enough to meet the girl he would marry. When Catherine
passed away in 1983, it seemed his dream would not come
true.

Then, while courting Nancy, he discovered that she, like
Catherine, was a graduate of Agnes Scott College; that
Nancy's mother and Catherine had served together on the
school's Board of Trustees; and, best of all, that Nancy, a
gifted communicator, too, had been Catherine's special
hostess one year at an Agnes Scott alumni gathering. So
Catherine and Nancy *had* met—not knowing, of course,
how the future would bring their two families together.

In June 1985, two years after Catherine's death, I married
Sandra Simpson, a joyous Christian, budding writer, and
mother of three children in their mid-twenties. Sandra's
book, *The Compulsive Woman*, was published in 1987 and
led us both into a ministry to compulsive-addictive people.
In the process, Sandy and I became aware that God had
further healing work for us to do in our own family relationships . . .

Sandy, with her children and their father. And I, with my
first wife, Eve.

When Linda called one day in the fall of 1988 to say she
planned to take sixteen-month-old Linda Whitaker to visit
Grandmother Eve, I found myself saying, "I'll go with you."

Like Catherine with Amy Catherine, I had tried unsuccessfully to understand why God had not healed Eve, who is now in a nursing home, unable to move about except in a wheelchair. All of us had maintained contact with Eve; the children had visited her; we had helped her financially. But it had been almost thirty years since I had seen Eve face-to-face.

When we arrived at the nursing home, Eve was sitting in her wheelchair finishing breakfast. Her body was ailing, but her face was alive, her eyes warm. The meeting was awkward at first, but not for long. Soon we were going back thirty years to reminisce over the good times we had had together.

There was no trace of bitterness in Eve, only gratitude. Gratitude that Catherine had been such a good mother to her children. (In fact, Eve had written to Catherine to express this.) Gratitude that her children had visited her in their adult years. Gratitude that her material needs had been provided for. I was astonished. Eve was blessing us.

We all went to church together and met Eve's friends; in fact, Linda and I were asked to stand and be introduced publicly during the service. It was a dramatic moment, as though we were acknowledging before the world our responsibility for our relationships and giving testimony to God's unlimited power to heal. Before our departure, the three of us held hands and prayed together while baby Whitaker played on the floor beside us. The healing tears flowed as we asked forgiveness for the hurts each one of us had brought on the others.

Later I reflected: Why do we underestimate the Lord's power to transform even the most damaged relationships?

Catherine held off raising the divorce issue in her writings because, although as recorded in her journals, she finally reached a point of peace about our situation, it was never clear to her what the meaning of her experience was for others. She was horrified at the thought that by disclosing the fact that she had married a divorced man, she might seem to be endorsing a practice she abhorred.

Today, when half of all marriages begun will end in divorce, many Christians are questioning whether biblical teaching on this subject is relevant to our times. To me, the dismal statistics seem ample reason for our society to return to scriptural principles regarding marriage and divorce. I was impressed by the total agreement in our family to cover the divorce issue in this book. "Bring it out in the open so people can see the anguish divorce brings," each member of the family concurred.

We also agreed that Jesus was concerned not with legalism, but with our well-being, when He spoke out so forcefully against divorce. Our Father in heaven wants to spare His children the grief, the pain, the spiritual and emotional damage that go with broken family situations.

The final truth is, of course, the forgiving, healing love of our Lord. He is in the business of repairing and restoring broken homes and hearts.

Catherine was His principal agent in my life and those of my children during our 23 years of marriage. She stepped into a chaotic home situation and welded five diverse personalities into a family. It was not a sense of her own adequacy that impelled her—on the contrary, she was all too aware of her shortcomings as a wife and mother. It was the certainty that God was adequate.

Throughout her life, in every tough situation—the loss of her husband, the challenge of single parenting, the death of two grandchildren, the clash of strong wills in a household—Catherine turned to her Redeemer. Even when He seemed farthest away, in the darkness of her own rebellion and alienation, she clung to the simple *fact* of His existence—in the absence of all feeling or evidence.

In Catherine's life He proved infinitely faithful. He longs to prove it in your life, too.